THE YOUNG ADULT'S LONG-DISTANCE RELATIONSHIP SURVIVAL GUIDE

Tips, Tricks and Expert Advice for Being Apart and Staying Happy

THE YOUNG ADULT'S LONG-DISTANCE RELATIONSHIP SURVIVAL GUIDE: TIPS, TRICKS AND EXPERT ADVICE FOR BEING APART AND STAYING HAPPY

Copyright © 2015 Atlantic Publishing Group, Inc.
1405 SW 6th Avenue · Ocala, Florida 34471 · Phone 800-814-1132 · Fax 352-622-1875
Website: www.atlantic-pub.com · Email: sales@atlantic-pub.com
SAN Number: 268-1250

Library of Congress Cataloging-in-Publication Data

Names: Atlantic Publishing Group, Inc.
Title: The young adult's long-distance relationship survival guide : tips,
    tricks and expert advice for being apart and staying happy / by Atlantic
    Publishing Group, Inc.
Description: Ocala : Atlantic Pub. Group, Inc., 2016. | Includes
    bibliographical references and index.
Identifiers: LCCN 2015041509 (print) | LCCN 2015045980 (ebook) | ISBN
    9781601389862 (alk. paper) | ISBN 1601389868 (alk. paper) | ISBN
    9781601389978 ()
Subjects: LCSH: Long-distance relationships. | Interpersonal relations in
    young adults. | Young adults--Life skills guides.
Classification: LCC HM1106 .Y68 2016 (print) | LCC HM1106 (ebook) | DDC
    302.34--dc23
LC record available at http://lccn.loc.gov/2015041509

Printed in the United States

Printed on Recycled Paper

Disclaimer

The material in this book is provided for informational purposes and as a general guide to the challenges and rewards of participating in a long-distance relationship.

Table of Contents

Chapter 2: Communication is the Key 29

Chapter 3: The Masks People Wear 65

Chapter 4: Setting Goals   77

Chapter 5: Be Great Solo and Together   93

Appendix   189

Index   195

Introduction

I
t is not difficult to spot a happy couple. The way they look at each other, the way they reach for each other's hands when walking down the street, and the way they seem oblivious to the world around them are all clues that these two people belong to each other.

What happens when there is no looking into each other's eyes, and there are no hands to hold when walking down the street? Is it possible to maintain a solid relationship when two people are separated by miles, time zones, and in some cases, an almost complete lack of communication for long periods? Can love continue despite distance?

The answer is "yes." Being in a long-distance relationship does not doom you and your boyfriend or girlfriend. Like any other successful relationship, these long-distance romances need attention to be successful. Although it is true that long-distance relationships can take a bit of effort, most relationships take effort. No relationship is without its difficulties, and just because miles separate you does not mean you cannot make it work.

These Relationships Can Work

Some people find that the time they spend away from their signaturing other strengthens the relationship. Think of relationships where two partners have never been apart. Do they know if they can trust each other when separated by miles? Do they know that old saying, "absence makes the heart grow fonder?" Do they know if they are strong as individuals and as a couple? People in successful long-distance relationships can boast these claims because they know them to be true from their own experiences.

CASE STUDY: LOVE CAN STAND THE TEST OF TIME

Ayana, married her long-distance sweetheart

I met my now-husband when I was 15 years old, and we started dating two years later. As luck would have it, he didn't ask me out until I moved away to attend college. We spent the next four years of our relationship long-distance, cherishing long weekends along with summer and winter breaks.

The hardest part at first was definitely learning to trust the other person. We were attending different schools about two hours away from each other — if either person wanted to stray from the relationship, the opportunity was there. A lot of our friends didn't get it — choosing exclusivity at 18 is one thing, but it sounds even crazier when the other person lives far away. There were times that we doubted we'd make it through the four years of college, and there were days where I cried because I missed him so much.

We downloaded countdown apps on our phones to keep track of how long we had until our next visits. For us, long distance was a blessing because it helped us maintain healthy boundaries and keep the promises we'd made to ourselves about waiting for marriage to live together and be intimate.

Toward the end of college, as many of my friends started pursuing long-term relationships, I'd many spend Friday nights in my apartment pretty bummed. I tried to channel the free time I had into good — I joined a sorority, took on several internships, and led a student club. I think that if we'd been in the same town, it would've been harder to make these goals a reality.

There were some positives. Because we didn't spend all of our time together, we got to develop our own friendships and lives outside of each other. We're less clingy than a lot of couples, because we know we can do weeks apart without a problem. And I never worry that he'll try to stop me

> from chasing my dreams — I was able to move across the country for a semester for my dream internship, and he's the one who told me to go for it.
>
> Our communication has improved as well. Because so many of our fights happened via text message and phone calls, we had to learn to fight fair — we didn't have the benefit of being able to make up in person. One of the sweetest parts of long distance, I think, is how much you appreciate the other person's presence once you're finally living in the same city.

When love endures physical time apart, it is a love that has been tested and will bode well for you as a couple in the future. Not all couples can say that their relationship overcame tough odds.

These Relationships Take Work

Long-distance relationships are not easy. It is hard being away from someone you love, and it can be difficult to dedicate yourself to someone whom you can't see every day. Reminders of your long-distance relationship are everywhere, whether you find yourself sitting alone at a party because your significant other is not around, "third-wheeling" with other couples, or you get upset watching a couple snuggle on a park bench.

Consider an example of a normal couple that sits together in a room doing homework separately. They are not necessarily interacting, but they are still together and are sharing an experience. Now, consider a couple in separate cities that is sitting in their own rooms doing homework. These two couples are engaged in the same act of highlighting and reading, but the couple in the same room gets to be physically close. Even as dull as the moment is, it strengthens the traditional couple, but for the long-distance couple, it becomes another afternoon of doing homework alone.

Long-distance relationships are not passive arrangements. For many people, however, love — or the possibility of love — is worth the extra effort. There are ways to change everyday moments like sitting and reading into one that helps strengthen your relationship, whether it is by sharing the moment using technology or learning how to effectively recharge your own batteries, so you have more strength to deal with having a loved one away.

This Book Will Help You Make It Work

This book presents advice from a different sources. You will read stories from people from different walks of life who have managed to make long-distance relationships work and from people who can look back and figure out why these relationships did not work for them. Expert advice also is provided throughout, so you will get the benefit of words of wisdom from couples that have been there and hear from relationship professionals who study the topic of long-distance relationships on an academic level.

This helpful guide will help you keep your relationship active, even from a distance. The importance of communication is stressed, and you will find ways to ensure that you present your true self to your boyfriend or girlfriend, even if it is over the phone, over the computer, or in person.

Use this book to help you and your partner set goals for your relationship and to spot when trouble is brewing (and how to stop trouble before it becomes big trouble). It will help you make your relationship succeed, even if you cannot spend time looking into each other's eyes or walking down the street hand in hand.

Chapter 1

Love Takes All Kinds

Not everyone in a long-distance relationship wants one. Although some couples make the decision to keep a relationship despite the miles, plenty of couples start out in traditional relationships and have to adjust to a long-distance arrangement because of circumstances beyond their control. No matter what the reason for the arrangement, being successful in a long-distance relationship takes extra effort.

Although there are not many formal studies regarding the number of couples currently involved in long-distance relationships, most estimates place the number of people in long-distance relationships to somewhere around 9 or 10 million. It is difficult to assess the number of people involved in long-distance relationships for several reasons. Relationships come and go, so this is not a constant number.

An informal study by the website **www.longdistancerelation ships.com** revealed some interesting statistics about people in long-distance relationships. Of the respondents (who were all involved in long-distance relationships when participating), the average distance between the partners was 125 miles. Long-distance couples visited each other one or two times a month, and when they called each other on the phone, they typically spent 30 minutes talking. The average duration of the long-distance arrangement among respondents was 14 months.

Your relationship might not fit within these statistics, and there is nothing wrong with that. Once you learn what works best for you and your boyfriend or girlfriend, you will have your guidelines on how your relationship best runs.

Is It Worth the Effort?

Nearly anyone who has been in a long-distance relationship knows how tough it can be to keep a relationship. Yet, plenty of couples start out — or wind up — in a long-distance relationship and manage to flourish. Being in a long-distance relationship has its unique issues, many of which quickly can evolve into full-blown problems. On the other hand, if you are in a long-distance relationship already, then you also realize that there is a reason you allow yourself to remain in this relationship despite the challenges. Whether you are convinced that you are with your soul mate, or you are so deeply invested in the relationship that ending things because of the distance is not an option, consider this time away from your partner to be a unique opportunity to prove your mutual commitment.

People from successful relationships commonly can reference a time in their relationship when they were tested. When a relationship can overcome the odds — such as when the relationship can withstand a long-distance arrangement — it serves as a potent reminder to the couple that they can get through things together.

 Quick Survival Tip

When you feel alone, physical distance does not change the love you and your partner feel for each other. Remind yourself that someone out there loves you and is willing to be with you despite the miles. When you think of things in those terms, it makes your relationship seem more incredible.

Make no mistake about it: Being in a long-distance relationship can be tough. Sometimes you just want someone to hug you and tell you everything is going to be fine after a long, hard day of classes or work. When it comes right down to it, however, if there is real potential for the relationship to be forever — or if you already know it is destined to be forever — then a long-distance arrangement is just another facet of your relationship to deal with.

CASE STUDY: MAKING IT WORK

Ashlee, not worried about the distance

I met Cody on prom night.

After the prom, I went to a friend's house, and across the street just so happened to be Cody's house. I had never met him before, but my friend swore that Cody and I would be perfect together. When I did not show the interest she was looking for in meeting Cody, she refused to get out of my car and demanded that I march over to Cody's house to meet him. So, there I went, in my prom dress, to meet Cody for the first time.

He was so sweet. We all hung out and after awhile, he offered to get me something comfortable to wear. He let me borrow a sweater and pajama pants, so I did not have to sit around in my prom dress. We hit it off right away, and I did not think twice about starting a relationship with him, even though we lived two hours away from each other. I already drove to his area about once a month to visit my friend, so as far as I was concerned, it was not unreasonable to think we could make it work.

The most difficult thing about being in a long-distance relationship was the time in between our visits, although the times when I had to leave to drive back home were a close second. I often wound up calling into work because I could not manage to leave Cody. On the bright side, I did get to concentrate on my schoolwork more when I was home because I was not with Cody. I also got to enjoy the time I had with him more than I might have if we lived close to each other. When we were together, it felt like a mini-vacation of happiness.

If I were to give advice to other people who are thinking about getting into a long-distance relationship, it would be this: Do what you want. If it is worth it to you, then it is worth doing. Cody and I are getting married in June of 2012; being his girlfriend while living two hours away was worth it for me.

How Did You Land Here?

Some couples have never known anything but a long-distance relationship, while others land in a long-distance relationship despite their best attempts to stay close to each other geographically. The difficulty of a long-distance relationship also can vary depending on the people involved. All long-distance relationships take work, but some scenarios can be tougher than others.

Separated by circumstances

Not everyone sets out to have a long-distance relationship. Sometimes circumstances occur that lead to a decision needing to be made: stay together long-distance or end the relationship? When you cannot make the choice to follow your partner for whatever reason, you might land unexpectedly in a long-distance relationship. The dynamics of the relationship can change drastically, and if both partners cannot adjust to the new arrangement, it can cause serious problems or prove to be the end of the relationship.

Extra tension in a relationship can occur when both partners do not necessarily agree about the arrangement. Suppose a boyfriend goes to college in another state, and this is after the girlfriend implored him not to, and she feared the distance would ruin the relationship. This relationship has to deal with the miles separating them and the underlying resentment both people might experience (him for feeling she did not support him, and her feeling he did not care enough to stay). Unless concerns are expressed and talked through, this couple will have the odds stacked against them. *You will learn more about the importance of communication — and how to leave the lines of communication wide open — in Chapter 3.*

Even when both people agree to maintain a long-distance relationship, and even when they are in total agreement about the circumstances leading up to the arrangement, extra tension can arise. Sometimes, it is just difficult to be alone, even in a relationship. One of the expectations for relationships includes companionship, and when your relationship does not provide companionship in the traditional way (hugging, smiles, etc.), it can make it a difficult arrangement.

CASE STUDY: SURVIVING MED SCHOOL

Gabrielle, starting a long-distance relationship with her long-time boyfriend

CLASSIFIED CASE STUDIES
™
directly from the experts

I'm 22 years old. I've been in a relationship for over seven years (I know, I know, we are one of those high school sweetheart couples that people can't believe still work). We went to high school and college together, lived in the same apartment complexes, and generally got to see each other whenever we wanted to. But "wanted" doesn't mean it actually happened. We have always been independent people. That meant we would go days without seeing each other despite living one floor apart.

When we started our long-distance relationship in January 2016, it wasn't so bad. He's in Gainesville, Florida, and I'm in Tampa. He hadn't started medical school, so we visited each other around three times a month.

Then, medical school started. We knew it would be hard and we were mentally prepared for it. If we expected to talk to each other every day and visit all the time, it would have been so much more difficult to cope. . I'm just starting out on this four-year stint of our long-distance relationship, so maybe I am naïve, but this system is working great for us. We see each other once or twice a month for about a day and a half at a time. And at those times he still has to study for a couple of hours, obviously. But what I can tell you is that "distance makes the heart grow fonder" is a VERY true clichéd statement.

Medical school is a true test for people in relationships. He is studying 24/7 and is constantly stressed out — everyone in medical school is (unless you're actually a savant for medicine). I talk to him an average of three minutes a day and definitely have gone days without getting to talk to him at all. And you have to understand — that is okay. Despite all of it, every time we see each other, it's a little bit sweeter.

Separated perpetually

It is common for two people to fall in love despite geographic distance. Whether the couple meets while one of them is just visiting or another circumstance, sometimes an attraction is too strong to ignore despite the distance. Couples who have an exclusive relationship, but who have never experienced anything but a long-distance relationship together, are at an advantage and a disadvantage. On the one hand, they do not know anything but the distance, so they cannot complain about how things once were because long distance has always been the norm for them. On the other hand, some might argue that it is nearly impossible to get to know someone well enough if they have never spent more than a few days in close proximity to each other.

Quick Survival Tip

If this is not your first long-distance relationship, acknowledge that every relationship is unique. Just because your previous relationship did not work, it does not mean that this relationship is doomed to fail, too.

These relationships have unique issues. How can you know that the image your partner presents to you is who he or she is, considering you have never had the opportunity to be with each other throughout a variety of situations? When you do not get the opportunity to witness how your partner reacts in times of stress, when upset, or when emotionally distraught, it can be difficult to get the big picture of whom that person is. Couples in this situation who flourish are those couples who communicate well and who do not put on masks to portray someone they are not. *You will learn more about the masks people wear in long-distance relationships in Chapter 4.*

CASE STUDY: MAKING IT WORK

Sara, college student

I suppose we were just at a point where it did not make sense to stay in the same city anymore — financially, career goals, etc. I feel lucky to be with someone committed enough to me and willing to be flexible. Breaking up was never discussed. We had been together for around a year when I graduated college, and he quit a job he did not like at all. At this point, we did not have any real direction for our relationship carved in stone. So, we decided that it was going to make the most sense long term to do things long-distance for a bit. We each moved back home with our parents. The way I picture it in my head sometimes — and what helps me deal with how much I miss him and all the other issues a long-distance relationship can bring — is sort of like a picture of the structure of DNA: together, split, together again. In this modern world, I imagine there are couples who have more (DNA transcription) bubbles than others, but perhaps shorter stretches (of nucleic acids) in between. If it is not yet obvious, I am a microbiology fan, so I cannot help but look at things in this way.

In our relationship, that is just it. We struggle with figuring out where and when the bubble will close up, and we will be able to be together again. Physically, that is. For us, there is not exactly a clear finish line in sight. At the same time, we are committed to making things work. So, for the past few months we have each made efforts to visit one another and stay connected every day. We have traveled and met in Washington, D.C., and he has visited me in my hometown of Omaha. I plan to visit him soon in California.

There is one big challenge: it is expensive. That is part of why we typically stay at our parents' houses or where we can secure free room and board. There are also issues of time — finding the time to talk on the phone when it is convenient in each of our schedules and with the time-zone difference. The problem of sheer absence makes keeping the fire hot (if you will) a little difficult, and we have to find creative ways to stay connected. We also have to relate to what each other and what we are doing independently. For lack of a more articulate way to put it, there are also times where I am tired, insecure, and sad, and it just sucks being apart.

We talk on the phone at least once a day. We also email and text things to each other at least once a day. We Skype when we can. Lately, we have been trying to make the same recipe for dinner once a week and video chat while we do so. Occasionally, we will send things to each other via snail mail: photos, postcards, and gifts. In general, I think we are pretty good communicators. We are honest and let each other know when something is bothering us. That is a good idea, long-distance or not.

I keep myself busy. Without us being in the same place, I do not feel pressure to cut back on certain commitments to make time for a dinner date, etc. At the same time, I realize I probably would not allow myself to be so busy if we were physically together and would make the time to spend with him instead of being so busy with my own things. Staying busy is absolutely a coping mechanism for me, as well as a way to save money to travel to visit him and open up options for us down the road. Other advantages — if you want to look at them this way — are that when we do finally get a chance to be together, it is more deliberate than ever, which is romantic. It forces us to plan to do things we may not have ever done otherwise if we were caught up in daily routines together and to attempt to not sweat the small stuff. If we have only a certain number of days together, we are not going to spend that time arguing. Even if we do disagree, we are more apt to resolve things and move on more quickly.

Support and Reactions

The type of long-distance relationship you have will affect the reaction you get from other people when talking about your partner. Couples who maintain long-distance relationships because their romance started online might feel the need to defend their relationship; even though more couples are meeting online, there can still be a stigma attached to online romances, which makes people apprehensive to talk openly about the difficulty of being apart.

The key is to have people you can talk to openly about the difficulties in maintaining a long-distance relationship, whether it is close friends, a support group, a parent, a licensed therapist, or someone else who is willing to help you deal with any relationship frustrations. This might take the form of a casual conversation over coffee riddled with venting frustrations or something more formal, where you talk with someone trained to assist people in your situation. Either way, seeking out support — regardless of the reasons for landing in a long-distance relationship — will be helpful if you seek help from the right people. *Chapters 5 and 6 will help you decide whom to turn to for help and who might not necessarily be looking out for your best interests.*

 Quick Survival Tip

There is no shame in turning to a therapist for help. Visiting a therapist does not mean there is something fundamentally wrong with you but instead just means you need a neutral person to listen to your feelings and ideas. Seek out a therapist who is well versed in helping people with long-distance relationships, and you will have a strong ally.

Banish negative talk

Guard your pessimistic thoughts and words that come out of your mouth. Suppose you try to call your partner, you receive his or her voice mail, and the intrusive and unfounded thought that he or she might be with another guy or girl pops into your mind. If you have no basis for this thought beyond receiving his or her voice mail, learn to banish this type of thought. On a similar note, do not accept these similar ideas from the people around you.

Why is it important not to allow your imagination to get the best of you when you are in a long-distance relationship? Long-distance relationships can work, but they take work. If you are in a long-distance relationship with someone whom you have committed to, or whom you think might be "The One," do not let miles be the end of your relationship. Instead, replace negative thoughts with positive ones, accept that your relationship will not be perfect, and move forward with your partner despite the physical distance. There is a chance the effort will be worth it in the end.

Chapter 2

Communication is the Key

One thing needs to be perfectly clear: Communication is a make-it-or-break-it factor in a long-distance relationship. This is not to say that limited communication will lead to the end of your relationship or that constant communication will guarantee a life of eternal love together. What it means is if you want to flourish in your long-distance relationship, you and your boyfriend or girlfriend must place communication high on your list of priorities.

Communication looks different for every long-distance couple and depends on a variety of factors. Being in a long-distance relationship does not doom you to having poor communication. Some couples live right next door to eachother yet do not spend time communicating. You can be in a long-distance relationship and still manage to have excellent communication with your partner, even if you hardly ever see each other in person.

This does not mean you and your partner have to speak to each other every day. It means the quality of your communication matters over the quantity. It will not help to chat with your partner for hours about the color you want to paint your bedroom walls when what you want to say is, "I feel lonely and need to know you still care about me."

Communication Will Make or Break a Relationship

The next time you have a conversation with someone face-to-face, pay attention to how much of the conversation is never spoken. So much communication is exchanged in a nonverbal way, whether it is a roll of the eyes or tensing of the body. People might say things their body language contradicts, and often, the nonverbal communication is the most accurate portrayal of the person's true feelings.

This is one of the reasons why communication in a long-distance relationship can be tough. When communication is reduced largely to email, texts, and phone calls, words and meanings might be misinterpreted. Suppose one person sends a text to his or her partner that says, "I wish I could be there for you the way your friends are." Depending on the context in which this text was sent and the way the recipient interprets this text, there could be myriad meanings behind what the text means.

The sender might have meant:

- "I appreciate that your friend was able to help you out when you needed a ride to the grocery store. I sometimes feel guilty that I cannot be there to help you, but it helps me feel better knowing there are other people who care about you and are willing to help you. We are lucky to have such friends."

- "I miss you, and I wish I was near you all the time. I would trade places with your friends if I could so I could hug you and see you."

- "I am resentful because you constantly complain that I am not there for you like your friends are. You already know that I cannot physically be there for you, but you continue to complain about it. Unfortunately, I cannot be there for you, and I wish you would stop complaining about it."

- "I think you are cheating on me with someone you claim is only a friend. I think it started because you were lonely and wanted someone to talk to, so you turned to this friend. I do not have proof though, so instead of blatantly accusing you cheating, I am going to drop passive-aggressive hints and hope this prompts you to tell me the truth. I'm just scared of losing you."

The recipient of the text does not have the advantage of seeing the sender's body language during this interaction, nor is the recipient even able to listen to the tone of voice of the sender. It is easy to tell when someone says something with the intention of portraying verbal irony; in this instance, if the sentence were said with a sneer, it would be obvious in the speaker's tone of voice. Text or email takes away the advantage of scrutinizing the other cues present beyond the face value of what the words are saying.

When your relationship is long distance, your communication with your partner will be via methods that are not face-to-face. There is also a chance you will not have the opportunity to communicate with your partner as much as you would like. When two people live in separate places, they have separate lives even if they are a couple. Much to the chagrin of the two people involved in a long-distance relationship, communication has to take a back seat to daily life.

Staying together when apart

Communication is important in any relationship, but when a relationship is long distance, communication might be one of the only ways the couple can stay connected. There are no flirtatious glances, quick squeezes of the hand, or opportunities to surprise each other with homemade treats or small gifts. These little things that serve as reminders that they enjoy a special connection are largely absent in a long-distance relationship, which makes communication more important. Think of communication as a way to stay connected.

A long-distance relationship is not going to thrive if there is little or no communication, especially if there was not a solid foundation for the couple in the beginning. Even the strongest relationships can suffer if communication is not sufficient when separated. Even if the couple has a strong bond to begin with, and even if they are in love with each other, the length of time with limited communication can cause an emotional distance that can turn into big problems if the couple is not able to reconnect when they are together again. Lack of communication causes issues, even with couples who do not have any other major problems.

Think of communication as a vital and necessary aspect to any long-distance relationship. Search for ways to keep communication open, and if necessary, cater to the communication styles that best suit both of you. For example, there are people who are eloquent in writing yet feel awkward when speaking on the telephone. There are people who would rather visit the dentist than sit in front of a computer and have a video chat session. Respect your partner's preferences when it comes to communicating, but make sure you also make your own preferences clear. Your partner might hate texting, but if you feel most loved when your partner sends a text or two a day to show that he or she is thinking about you, make it clear that you appreciate the effort it takes your partner to send those daily texts. You also might feel an elevated sense of closeness with a partner who is willing to step outside his or her comfort zone to make you feel special.

Set clear expectations for communication in your long-distance relationship. If you expect your partner to call you every night to wish you sweet dreams — and if it is feasible for your partner to do this — let your partner know that this is your expectation and is something you will expect unless your partner tells you otherwise. Your partner might not even realize the vital importance of these phone calls before bed, so the first time your partner forgets to call before going to sleep, you might panic and think this must be a sign your relationship is deteriorating. In reality, your partner just fell asleep before calling and did not realize this would cause such emotional distress.

Do you see how this scenario quickly might evolve into a huge fight? You call your partner demanding to know why you did not receive your nighttime phone call, and your partner is so thrown off by your emotional outburst that he or she reciprocates by saying you are too controlling. Your partner does not understand why he or she is suddenly getting yelled at. You cherish the nightly telephone calls, and you were hurt when you did not get your call, but emotions can cloud the truth when communication is not open and honest.

If you have any hope of flourishing in a long-distance relationship, one thing is essential: Do not expect your partner to be able to read your mind. Communicate how you feel and what you expect. Although some partners might be able to notice subtle hints regarding what the other partner wants based on nonverbal communication, you do not have this advantage when involved with someone long distance. If you want a nightly phone call, tell your partner that. Do not hint that you want a nightly phone call, complain that you feel particularly lonely before bed, or just not say anything and stew silently about how your partner cannot sense you want to receive a phone call every night. This is not fair to you, and it is not fair to your partner.

Communication does not come easily for everyone. You or your partner might have grown accustomed to not speaking your mind or saying things just to keep everyone else happy. This is common with people who have a desire to please everyone or who do not feel confident enough to reveal what they want and expect. Some people do not know what they want, so they do not feel they are in any position to tell other people what they want. Being in a long-distance relationship is not the time to keep your feelings to yourself. If anything, be more verbal and clear about what you want and what you expect from your partner.

Questions to ask yourself and your partner

Ask yourself these questions to prepare yourself to communicate more effectively with your long-distance partner, and then ask your partner to answer the questions, too. You might be surprised by the answers.

- When do I feel most loved?

- When do I feel most vulnerable or uneasy?

- What are the best ways for my partner to demonstrate love and affection from afar?

- What are some deal breakers for this relationship? Deal breakers are things that you cannot put up with that would likely cause the end of the relationship.

- What is my favorite form of communication with my partner?

- What is my least favorite form of communication with my partner, and how can I make it more enjoyable?

- Am I a decent communicator?

- Do I sometimes say things that I do not mean?

- What can I do to improve communication in my long-distance relationship?

The act of communicating comes easily to most people. The majority of people do not have trouble calling a pizza place to order a delivery or conveying to a friend what a movie was about. Communication can get tricky when emotions are involved, and the trickiness increases when the person you are talking to is hardly ever around. Consider communication in your long-distance relationship to be important and worthy of working on to ensure you have the best communication possible with your partner. It might be the thing that takes your long-distance relationship from a maybe-forever status to a definite-forever status.

Quick Tips for Making Communication a Priority

Making sure communication is a priority in your long-distance relationship does not have to be a daunting task, especially if you and your partner seem to be on the same page with most things. You already might have a rapport with your partner that allows both of you to speak your mind and clearly state what your expectations are. If this is the case, you just might need to work on staying connected and keeping communication open. If, on the other hand, you and your partner routinely misinterpret each other and find that mixed communication is a recurring theme in your arguments, then make a concerted effort to improve your communication to give your long-distance relationship a chance to flourish.

Convey your needs

If you have ever wished that your partner knew how you felt or what you were thinking, take solace in the fact that you are not the only person with that wish. The easy way to remedy this problem is to open up communication and tell your partner how you feel and what you are thinking.

Do you want your partner to tell you that you are attractive? Instead of hinting around, tell your partner it means something to you when he or she tells you how attractive you are. If all else fails, ask your partner, "Do you think I am attractive?" It is not fishing for a compliment and you shouldn't feel shallow for asking. It's simply a way for you to feel more secure.

Discover your partner's needs

You might have at one point wished you could crawl into your partner's head and figure out what was going through his or her brain. You do not have to resort to such measures when you ask what is going on. Although your partner might not be comfortable sharing every detail of his or her thoughts, the fact that you care enough to ask — and listen to the answer — fosters an open communication environment in the relationship. Listening is just as important as sharing.

Avoid communication overdose

Communication is important in a long-distance relationship, but so is being cognizant of your partner's feelings. You do not have to describe every detail of your trip to the mall, especially if you have limited time to spend on the phone or computer with your partner. If you talk or write too much, your partner might start to tune you out. Do not fall into the trap of communicating just for the sake of communicating. In other words, know what bores your partner, and avoid it. If you are not sure what bores your partner, ask. If the two of you have open communication, this should be an enlightening conversation. On the other hand, if you are reluctant to ask your partner to list what topics bore him or her, or if you are pretty sure that your partner would care more about sparing your feelings instead of telling you the truth about what topics are boring, pay attention to your partner's reactions. Use your observations to figure out what topics seem to make your partner lose interest. Does your partner start mumbling "uh-huh" a lot when you start talking about your favorite sports team? Does your partner seem distracted when the topic of your shoe collection comes into the conversation? These are relatively reliable indications that you have lost your partner's interest.

Jump over communication hurdles

If you never get face-to-face time with your partner to talk, use a phone. There are so many easy ways to communicate through apps, such as Snapchat and WhatsApp. If you or your partner does not have ready access to a phone (which is a crazy thought in this day and age), use email. If phone and email are not options, communicate the old-fashioned way and resort to written letters sent through the mail. Communication should be a priority in your long-distance relationship. Do not allow a hurdle to stop you from communicating with your partner.

Adjust as needed

Do not be afraid to try new ways of communicating. As technology evolves, so do the methods available for staying in touch with people far away. If you are not a fan of one particular method of communicating, let your partner know how you feel and suggest alternatives for staying in touch. Be aware of your partner's preferences for communication as well. You do not want to disregard one method of communication completely if it is your partner's favorite way of talking to you.

 Quick Survival Tip

I am not the biggest fan of video chat when the Internet connection is slow, as is the case sometimes when chatting online with someone in an overseas location. I prefer instant messaging, and luckily, my partner understands the frustration I feel when sitting through a bad connection on video chat does not help our communication.

Keep communication center stage

Some people grow accustomed to their long-distance relationship and forget to work at staying connected to their partner. Periodically review the communication between you and your partner. Are you both covering important things when you talk? Are you conveying your genuine feelings to your partner, while also asking to hear about his or her genuine feelings? Do not allow communication to fall by the wayside.

Communication includes listening

Communication is not all about telling your partner how you feel; it is also about listening to the things your partner says. This does not mean waiting for your partner to finish talking, so you swiftly can move on to the next thing you want to talk about. This means truly listening to your partner and understanding the things he or she says. There is a chance this is what you expect from your partner, so you should work on respecting eachother.

Active listening

Listening is crucial in a long-distance relationship, but it becomes even more important when the two of you are having a serious discussion or an argument. Active listening involves acknowledging what your partner has said before moving on with what you want to say. This ensures you actually understood the meaning of what your partner was trying to convey instead of hearing something else entirely. When communication takes place via telephone or email, it can be difficult to glean the actual meaning of what your partner is trying to get across. It becomes even more difficult when you are trying to discuss something emotional or something you do not necessarily agree on. Your interpretation of what your partner is trying to say might be skewed by what you *think* your partner is trying to say.

Here is an example of a typical conversation, followed by how active listening might help clarify the conversation for the two people involved.

Person 1: *I cannot believe you forgot about our lunch date.*

Person 2: *I was busy.*

Person 1: *We made these plans weeks ago! You never have time for me.*

Person 2: *I have classes! I cannot just drop everything and scamper off to lunch with you when I have work to do.*

Here is the same conversation, but with active listening, there is a better chance that this conversation will not end in one or both partners walking away from the conversation angry.

Person 1: *I cannot believe that you forgot about our lunch date.*

Person 2: *I hear you saying that you are upset that I forgot about our lunch date.*

Person 1: *Yes, that is what I am saying.*

Person 2: *I understand that you are upset. I am sorry that I upset you because that is not what I intended.*

Person 1: *I hear you apologizing, and I appreciate the apology.*

Person 2: *I want you to understand that school has been really hectic for me lately, and I feel a lot of pressure from you to follow whatever schedule you put into place for me.*

Person 1: *So, you are saying that I put too much pressure on you? I just want to have time with you.*

Person 2: *I know that you want to spend time with me. I am not saying that I do not want to spend time with you. Instead, I am saying that I need a little more leeway nowadays with my hectic schedule.*

Person 1: *I hear you saying that you do want to spend time with me, but I need to try to be flexible with my demands on your time. Is that right?*

Person 2: *Yes, that is what I am trying to say. Please understand that I really do want to spend time with you. I feel horrible about forgetting our lunch date.*

Person 1: *I want to spend time with you too. How about you look at your schedule and let me know when lunch will work with your schedule?*

Person 2: *That sounds great.*

Active listening can sound a little robotic or scripted, but it is not a technique to be used all the time. This is a common technique used by couples counselors to ensure both people involved in the conversation get their points across successfully before moving along in the conversation. It allows both people to clarify points as necessary, and nobody walks away from the conversation wondering what the other person was saying. It also keeps the emotional response to a minimum because both people in the conversation are forced to be logical and analytical. Try using the active listening technique the next time you have to discuss something sensitive with your partner. When serious conversations have to take place from a distance, helping techniques like active listening can make the conversation go much more smoothly.

"I" versus "You"

A common mistake couples make when having heated conversations is to shift the focus off "I" and onto "You." For example, instead of saying "I am hurt because you forgot our lunch date," you might say, "You do not care about me enough to remember our lunch date." Instead of effectively conveying your feelings, this results in you forcing the blame onto your partner while also attacking his or her commitment to you. It is one thing to be upset that your partner forgot about your lunch date, but it is another thing entirely to accuse your partner of not caring about you. Even if there is truth to the accusation of your partner not caring about you as much as you would like, focus on the topic at hand, and deal with the bigger problems when the time is right.

One of the easiest ways to make sure your conversation stays on topic is to start your sentences with the phrase "I feel." This will keep you from attacking your partner while also giving you the opportunity to get your point across. So, instead of "If you cared about me you would have made time for me," it instead becomes, "I feel hurt that you forgot about our lunch date." The second sentence directly addresses your feelings and gives your partner the opportunity to respond. The first sentence has the potential to allow the conversation to veer off in an unattended direction, never really allowing the actual problem to get resolved or even addressed.

You cannot assume what your partner is feeling. Do not tell your partner that his or her feelings are invalid because feelings often are emotionally driven and hard to define to begin with. Saying something to your partner along the lines of "Your feelings are wrong" can be a damaging statement. Focus on your own feelings and effectively conveying those feelings to your partner in your conversation. Combine this technique with the effective listening techniques, and your difficult conversations can be productive and resolved even when you cannot have the conversation face-to-face.

Absolutes

One more important thing to remember when trying to effectively communicate with your partner is to avoid absolute statements. Absolutes refer to words like "never" or "always." For example, if you tell your partner he or she never listens to you, you are putting an absolute within your claim that invalidates the entire statement. It cannot be true that your partner never listens to you. If it were true, what would be the point in making the statement in the first place?

When you make an absolute statement, what you are actually trying to convey is something emphatic. You emphatically believe that in some instances, your partner does not listen to what you say. Although this might be true, it is certainly not the same as making the statement that your partner never listens to you. When you put it in absolute terms, you lose your credibility in the assertion. Your partner will not hear your feelings or frustrations in that statement; instead, your partner will hear only the accusation. Do not be surprised if this elicits an angry response from your partner.

When having a serious discussion or argument with your partner, avoid absolutes because they are seldom true. Do not mask absolutes in discussions of your feelings, either. In other words, just because you start the sentence "you never listen to me" with "I feel," it does not make it any more effective when trying to resolve the issue. Instead, say, "I feel as though there are some times when you do not listen to me," which is probably much more accurate than "You never listen to me."

Arguments happen

You are not going to be able to avoid arguments altogether. *You will learn more about fighting fairly later in this chapter.* When you are in a long-distance relationship, the need for effective communication becomes even more important, so you can both feel as though you are on the same page despite the distance. Although it might feel odd to bring communication tools into heated conversations, the result is a more constructive conversation that builds the connection between the two of you. You may not like the idea of following rules when trying to resolve a problem, but these rules will help you both resolve the issue instead of dancing around the topic or getting so angry that you just glaze over the whole thing.

Once you and your partner become accustomed to using active listening and the other tips listed above, your arguments probably will start to evolve into discussions intended to solve the problem instead of turning into heated arguments that do not solve anything. Active listening and the other techniques become habits when you use them frequently, and these techniques can take your long-distance relationship to the next level.

Quick Survival Tip

Active listening has to be something that the two of you agree to use. It will not work if only one of you is using this technique during a heated discussion.

Options for Long-Distance Communication

Not long ago, a long-distance relationship was doomed to only using telephone or mail for communication, and although these options were better than no communication, technology has blessed long-distance couples with the ability to stay in touch through a wide variety of methods. Depending on where you and your partner are, a long-distance relationship might not even seem that far removed from any other relationship, particularly if you are in the position to contact your partner any time, no matter where he or she is. Being able to see your partner — even if it is on a computer screen or using video chat on your phone — can make him or her seem not so far away.

Letters

Do not automatically dismiss the idea of writing letters to your partner while he or she is away from you. Although writing letters might seem like an old-fashioned method of communicating, many people feel it is a lost art that recipients still appreciate.

A letter says more than what is written on the page. A letter says, "I took the time to sit down and write this with my own hands because you are worth the time and effort it took to compose this letter." Receiving a letter in the mail — especially if it is unexpected — can be a real treat for your boyfriend or girlfriend. Handwritten letters are not so common anymore, so this makes this method of communication all the more special.

If it has been a long time since you wrote a letter, rest assured that it is not a complicated process, and your partner is not expecting perfection (if he or she is even expecting a letter). If you have trouble thinking of things to write, try starting out with these ideas:

- Write a letter about how lucky you are to have your partner and why.

- Write about a special memory you have about the two of you, such as when you first met or when you first realized your partner was special.

- Write about something funny that happened in your day.

- Write about the dreams you have of what you will do the next time you are together or what the future holds for you both.

In a situation where your partner is temporarily away but will eventually return, consider including newspaper clippings or photos of things going on around town, so your partner can feel more connected to the community, despite being far away. This particularly is welcome if your partner is somewhere different from what he or she is used to. There are resources to help you with sending letters if you have a hard time composing something. Look through the greeting card section the next time you are shopping to see what cards are available; you might be surprised by the vast variety of "Miss You" cards that do not need more than a signature and a stamp. If you are under the impression that all greeting cards are sappy, there is a chance you will encounter other types of cards, including funny cards and romantic cards, but not in a sappy way.

Greeting cards should help your correspondence but not replace your correspondence altogether. Receiving a greeting card every week with nothing more than a quick signature from a partner might make the recipient feel like there is not enough effort being put into staying in touch. So, although there are ways to help you send notes to your partner through the mail, put effort into the process, and do not rely solely on greeting cards to convey your feelings to your partner.

Quick Survival Tip

Letters sent through the mail may seem outdated, but do not discount the power of an unexpected letter.

Telephone

Hearing your partner's voice is important and special, even when the two of you cannot be in the same room. You are familiar with your partner's unique speech patterns and can tell by the inflections in your partner's voice where the emphasis is on what your partner is saying. When you are in a long-distance relationship, your phone can be one of the most important tools you use to stay connected.

There are practical considerations you and your partner should keep in mind when using the telephone to keep in touch.

- Review your parent's telephone service plan. It would be a rude surprise for your parents to receive a cell phone bill that is triple what they are used to paying because you thought you had unlimited minutes but did not. If you know you are going to spend hours chatting with your partner, make sure your telephone plan can support it.

- Set clear expectations with your partner for how often you will talk via telephone and at what times. This does not mean you cannot be spontaneous and call your partner unexpectedly to say you are thinking about him or her, but be realistic in your expectations. This means that if your partner is not allowed to use the phone while working, you will not leave 12 angry voice mails because your partner did not answer the phone at work. Be practical. Your partner is not at your beck and call, no matter how much in love the two of you are.

- Respect each other's preferences for talking on the phone. Maybe you only like to talk when there is a definitive topic at hand, but your partner can easily spend three hours on the phone talking about nothing in particular. The phone should be a tool to keep the two of you together and not a tool to distance you.

Do not allow these guidelines to stop you from having natural telephone conversations that occur organically. You do not want to be so focused on the practicality of phone conversations that you forget what a decent tool the phone is for staying connected. Your partner cannot be there for you all the time by phone, and you have to be all right with this.

You can use the phone to have a "date" with your partner when you watch a television show, eat dinner, or even go to (separate) coffee shops together. These telephone dates are an excellent way to feel connected to your partner despite the distance. *In Chapter 7, you will learn more about having a phone date with your long-distance partner.*

If you are in a situation where telephone calls are rare (such as is the case with couples in vastly different time zones), the importance of coordinating a time for a phone conversation is increased. It can be frustrating to miss a call from your long-distance partner, but when you realize you have missed a call after not having spoken to your partner in a while and will not hear from your partner again for a while, this can shake you to the core. You might feel inadequate because you missed the call or allow your feelings to make you feel you have let your partner down by not sitting by the phone awaiting a call. If you accidentally miss a phone call from your partner — even if your partner rarely has access to a phone — do not allow yourself to dwell on it to the point where you feel horrible or inadequate as a partner. Feel guilt if you are intentionally avoiding phone calls from your partner, but not if you just miss a phone call.

When you are talking to your partner over the phone, listen to what he or she says and how he or she says it. It is one thing to say, "I miss you, too," but it is another thing when this is said distractedly or in a sarcastic tone. You do not have the benefit of seeing your partner's face during a phone conversation; so if you need clarification on something your partner has said, ask. It is better to make sure you understand what your partner is saying instead of walking away from the conversation more confused.

Texting

Texting is good for passing along chunks of information, such as, "Just thought you should know I am thinking about you" or "Please remember Katy's party on Saturday." Some long-distance couples enjoy having conversations via text because they are instantaneous and can be snuck in when a telephone conversation cannot. For example, a person riding in the car on the way to school might not be comfortable with having a telephone conversation, but texting is a private situation and can happen while surrounded by people without sharing what is being said.

As with telephone conversations, there are practical considerations when texting with your long-distance partner.

- Not all cell phone providers automatically offer unlimited texts. Find out what your parent's cell phone plan says about texts, and if you know you will be texting with your partner, figure out the best way to make this an inexpensive option. Apps can also be used.

- Texts can be saved and shared with other people. Keep in mind that once something is sent, there is no way of undoing it.

- The way things are written sometimes does not effectively convey what it is you are trying to say. Even though texts are relatively quick methods of communication, reread — and maybe even speak aloud — what you have written to make sure there is nothing that could be misinterpreted.

Quick Survival Tip

Auto-correct, which is a cell phone's way of ensuring you spell everything correctly in the body of your text, can be just as annoying as it is convenient. If you are not careful, auto-correct might completely change the meaning of your text. My friend sent me a text inviting me to karaoke, and the next text said, "I want to cuddle with you." It turns out she was trying to say, "I want to sing with you," but the auto-correct stepped in when she mis-spelled the word "sing." We had a laugh about that one, but it was an excellent example of how texting can warp intended communication. For more examples, check out **http://damnyouautocorrect.com**.

Texting should not be a replacement for real conversation unless texting is your only option for staying in touch with your partner. Text conversations can get disjointed, and the necessary for these conversations can halt progress if you are trying to have a serious conversation about your relationship or something else important. Consider texting to just be another communication tool, but not the preferred method of staying in touch.

You will learn about fighting fairly with your long-distance partner later in this chapter, but for now just remember that texting is not an effective method for having an argument with your partner. Texts are too abrupt and too restrictive to use for fighting, and it is generally inadvisable to use texts for having a heated discussion. If a text conversation seems to be evolving into an argument, agree to put the discussion on hold until you have the opportunity to speak about your differing points of view over the phone or in person, if possible.

Your partner has a life, too. If you send a text and do not receive an immediate response, this does not automatically mean you are being ignored. Your partner cannot always drop everything and respond to your text. If this is the case, do not allow yourself to be hurt or offended. It is one thing if your partner is truly ignoring you, but it is another thing if he or she is just busy.

Texting should be one of the several methods for communication you use to stay connected to your partner. Unless there is a particular reason why this is the only way the two of you can communicate, it should not be your main method.

Email

Email is to society what written letters once were. There is a chance you are comfortable with how email works. The advantages to email is that it is delivered right away to your partner's inbox, and you can revise your draft several times before you send it to make sure you are getting your point across without any confusion.

Sending email once a day, if possible, can be nice. However, this depends on your preferences and capabilities. You might not have the time to send email every day, just as you might not enjoy the process of composing email and find a once-a-day email obligation to be daunting. A daily email can help because it is a predictable communication schedule and something that can be saved. When a partner is away from the person he or she loves, having a folder of email to read when he or she wants is a motivator and reminder of the love between both partners.

Some of the same rules for written letters apply for email. Reread what you write to make sure everything is clear, and there is no confusion as to what you are trying to say. Email is not the place for blatant accusations or angry assaults. Fighting fairly will be discussed later in this chapter, but that email is one-sided. In a face-to-face conversation, both people can defend themselves if necessary. In an email format, if a long list of complaints is aired, this is more of a complaint letter than a correspondence between loving couples.

You might not have any other choice but to resort to email for your communication with your partner, depending on your situation. If this is the case, once the email is sent, there is no getting the email back. So, if you send a long, angry email to your partner accusing him or her of not being faithful (or whatever else is on your mind when you type the email), there no way to erase what you wrote after you sent the email, and your partner can keep the email. Heated conversations can fade in memory over time, but an angry email can be reread forever.

Video chat

One of the best technologies available for long-distance couples is video chat, which allows you to see your partner while talking to him or her. This is available over the Internet and with phones that have video chat capability. With video chat, you have the advantage of being able to see your partner during the conversation. This erases the issue of not being able to see your partner's body language, which can help your communication immensely.

Not everyone is comfortable with video chat. For some, the thought of cameras trained on their faces makes them nervous and might compel them to act unnaturally. Video chat is not perfect; the quality of the video chat is largely dependent upon the Internet connection and the quality of the webcam used.

On the other hand, video chat is popular and widely available. Skype, which is one of the most popular methods for video chat available on the Internet, provides a simple setup process and is free to use.

Here are other interesting facts about Skype:

In 2010:

- Skype-to-Skype voice and video minutes totaled about 531 million minutes per day (194 billion minutes for the year).

- Skype-to-Skype and Skype to land lines/mobile voice and video minutes totaled about 207 billion minutes.

- Users sent more than 176 million SMS text messages through Skype.

At peak times, about 30 million concurrent users are logged into Skype at any given time (as of March 2011).

- Video Calling:

  o In the first half of 2011, video calls accounted for about 43 percent of Skype-to-Skype minutes.

  o At peak times, about half a million simultaneous video calls are made on Skype (as of June 2011).

  o Peak video minutes occur on Sunday afternoons (GMT).

  o On average, more than 4,000 hours of video is transmitted every minute on Skype (as of May 2011).

  o About 75 percent of Skype's online users have made a video call.

  o Skype users make an average of 300 million minutes of video calls per day (connected users as of June 2011).

Video Chat helps to be able to see loved ones, even if it is not face-to-face. For someone who is perpetually away, video chat is the next best thing to being in the same room with a partner.

Although video chats do not result in transcripts of the conversation like texting, instant messaging, and emails can, most video chat programs have recording capabilities. Whether a screenshot (a frozen picture of a moment in the video chat) or a full recording of the entire conversation, keep in mind that your conversation might not remain private. Most employers reserve the right to monitor employee activities on company computers, and in certain instances, computer activity might be monitored for security reasons. Even if you completely trust your partner, computers are not necessarily trustworthy. So, although you do not have to censor yourself too much or present yourself as someone other than who you are while in a video chat, think twice before making any rash decisions.

If possible, schedule recurring video chats with your partner. This is dependent on whether you both enjoy the video chat process, and it might take time before video chatting becomes a smooth process for both of you. If both of you can fall into a pattern of having video chats once or twice a week, this can be an excellent method for you to connect with each other despite the miles. Some long-distance couples try to video chat at least once a day, and sometimes more than once a day.

Work with What You Have

If you are in the fortunate position of having access to these communication tools, you have the ability to choose what works best for you and your partner. There is a chance you will settle on one main method of communication while utilizing the other forms available. The point is to stay in touch and stay connected. Long-distance relationships have a difficult time flourishing if the communication is not there.

CASE STUDY: MILITARY RELATIONSHIP

Makenzi, going the distance with a U.S. Army soldier

Starting in our senior year in high school, we were together on and off for the following two and a half years. Then, my soldier graduated boot camp, and the story of our long-distance relationship began: U.S. Army edition. Being in a long-distance relationship is challenging, and being in a long-distance relationship that involves the military can be that much more difficult.

I am a senior in college in south Florida and my fiancé is a soldier. He was first stationed in South Carolina, then in Georgia for training, and is now currently stationed in Texas where he is facing a rapidly approaching deployment in February of 2017. On average, I have seen him once every three months between multiple seven-hour drives to Georgia and now three trips to Texas. Being separated most of the time has made those trips as valuable as gold, and I am eager to see him again in another nine weeks.

I am often asked, "How do you do it?" My best answer is that I don't know — I just take it one day at a time. FaceTime has been the biggest lifesaver. It's the closest thing we can do to make it seem like we're together, and it makes coping with the distance so much easier. Sometimes we won't speak for days because our schedules can be conflicting and time zones become a real issue too. I also keep a countdown until I see him next —it helps to actually watch the time wind down.

Being separated has also allowed us to work on the weaknesses in our relationship. In the beginning, for example, my fiancé was not efficient in communicating how he felt, especially when it was something he had a problem with. It was a learning experience for both of us to be able to discuss problems that we had in order to reach common ground.

Although I am ready to be closer to him, being in a long-distance relationship has been one of the best things I have done for myself as well as for my relationship. I have found that many people get into relationships and attach themselves to their partner and allow their lives to become one instead of a collaboration of two lives. I have been able to work on my ability to be independent and make myself happy while working on my career until we are finally able to be together. Maintaining a full and independent lifestyle while in a long-distance relationship is the best thing you can do for yourself.

My soldier and I have another year or so until I can finally move to Texas, but I know that I can look forward to future learning experiences with my best friend. As hard as it may be, I know that the distance is only temporary, and I want to keep him in my life forever. So for now, I will wait as patiently as I can. It doesn't get easier; you just get stronger.

Fighting Fairly

You are going to argue with your partner. Arguing is a staple of any relationship. Two people bring their own thoughts and feelings into the relationship, and it is unlikely that people will always agree about everything that comes up. Arguing is not unhealthy in a relationship, but much depends on how the fighting takes place. When an argument is resolved after both people have aired their feelings and a compromise results from the discussion, this serves to strengthen the relationship. It is when arguments become opportunities to try to hurt each other — or competitions to see who can be crowned "right" — that arguments take an ugly turn and wind up damaging the relationship.

There is a chance you have encountered arguments in a face-to-face setting, but the rules for fighting fairly change when you are in a long-distance relationship. This does not mean it is necessary for you to hold in your feelings or just accept undeserved criticism from your long-distance partner. Instead, the point is to communicate your concerns effectively while also effectively listening to what your partner has to say.

Insecurities

Trying to trust someone you do not see on a regular basis can cause insecurities to grow. This can be a big problem with long-distance relationships, but as long as the two people involved acknowledge insecurities and do not attempt to mask these feelings as something else, it does not have to mean the end to the relationship. When insecurities are masked as something else, they might take the form of anger, jealousy, or even doubt. You feel insecure with your relationship because you know your partner hangs out with a wide variety of people and worry your partner will like someone else. Instead of voicing your insecurities in a reasonable way, such as, "I worry you will become attracted to someone you're hanging out with because you hardly get to see me," you might wrap your insecurities up in a blanket of other emotions, so you do not feel as vulnerable. An example of this is, "Why couldn't you answer your phone when I called? Were you too busy with friends? You do not even care about me, do you?"

Say what you mean, and acknowledge that there will be times when you feel insecure in your long-distance relationship. There will be times when your partner cannot answer the phone or when an email is not responded to as quickly as usual. When these instances occur, insecurities might pile up and might even be the end of the relationship. Instead, acknowledge insecurities and discuss them with your partner. Wording is important here, especially when talking about issues involving trust. Instead of saying, "I have a hard time shaking the idea that you are cheating on me," which sounds like an accusation, try something along the lines of, "When you are away, my insecurities get the best of me, and I worry that you might find someone else," which puts the blame for the insecurities on you instead of your partner. Unless you have a valid reason for thinking your partner is with someone else, avoid throwing the "cheating card" into a conversation when there is no real reason for it.

Be fair

When you acknowledge that there are bound to be insecurities in a long-distance relationship and that it is best to be honest and open about your feelings instead of allowing your feelings to explode out in a twisted form, it becomes clear that certain behaviors will do nothing but damage your relationship. For example, hanging up on your partner in a phone conversation can do even more harm in a long-distance relationship than it will in a traditional relationship. It is similar to walking away from a heated conversation, but when your primary method of communication is by telephone, it has the potential to cause additional problems or maybe even create a stigma that telephone conversations have the potential to turn sour. Telephone conversations that end abruptly in anger leave both partners feeling upset and perhaps even reluctant to pick up the phone again in the future. In this particular instance, it would be far better to tell your partner, "I am angry right now, so I need to end this conversation, but I will call you after I have had a chance to cool down."

It might seem like the examples of things to say place the blame squarely on your shoulders, and this is true. Keep in mind that you are driven by your own emotions, and for that reason you have to take responsibility for them. You might think to yourself, "He makes me so mad," but it is more accurate to say, "I allow myself to get mad." Nobody can force you to feel a certain way; you have to take ownership of your responses. Instead of placing the blame on your partner for your emotions, be fair, and acknowledge that these are your emotions and that you are responsible for them.

Justified fighting

Arguments are going to happen, and sometimes these arguments are completely justified. If resolved to the satisfaction of both people, arguments actually can serve to strengthen a relationship. There can be something incredibly powerful about knowing that a disagreement can be faced head-on and eventually resolved; it lets both people in the relationship know that a simple argument is not going to be the end. When you are in a long-distance relationship, the stronger your bond is, the stronger your chance is of staying together despite the distance.

What happens if you or your partner does something that results in a big blow-up? When a huge, heated argument occurs — especially when it happens by phone or over the computer — it can be difficult to keep your emotions in proper perspective. Your mind might say, "I am frustrated, angry, and hurt," but your mouth might say, "You are the worst boyfriend/girlfriend ever, and I hate you." The nonverbal cues that might prompt you to react a certain way are absent, so, it might be even easier to allow your emotions to bubble over and explode. After all, there is a big difference between hearing your partner say, "I am sorry" over the phone or computer and seeing your partner say these words.

Here are tips for arguing fairly when in a long-distance relationship:

- Say what you mean. Your partner cannot read your mind, especially from miles away.

- Examine your emotions, and do not blame your partner for your own feelings.

- Do not allow your imagination to make the situation worse. Just because your partner does not answer the phone, it does not automatically mean your partner is cheating.

- Consider your partner's feelings. Hanging up on your partner or abruptly ending a computer conversation can make things worse.

- Keep in mind that the goal is not to avoid arguments entirely, but instead, it is to fight fairly and resolve issues in a way that will strengthen the relationship.

You will learn more about how to avoid sabotaging your relationship in the Chapter 9. Unfortunately, for many long-distance couples, they fall into the trap of sabotaging their relationships and wind up breaking up. You do not have to fall into this pattern. No matter what your specific situation, you can make your long-distance relationship work.

Chapter 3

The Masks People Wear

Who are you? This is a loaded question, but it is an important question to ask when dealing with any relationship, especially a long-distance relationship. Sometimes being in a relationship where most of the communication takes place over the phone or computer can make it too easy to present yourself as someone other than who you truly are. This can happen without you even realizing it. Think about which parts of you are exposed to your partner. Do you only share happy stories when chatting on the telephone, or do you omit problems when emailing your partner? By only presenting a perpetually happy version of yourself to your partner, you are putting on a happy mask that can cause big problems when the two of you are able to spend time together.

It can be difficult to be yourself when the majority of your communication with your partner is not face-to-face. When you are in a traditional relationship, your partner sees your emotional outbursts when something goes wrong, but in a long-distance relationship, you might censor these outbursts before contacting your partner. Although you certainly do not want to overwhelm your boyfriend or girlfriend with everything that goes wrong throughout your day, you do not want to make everything seem so wonderful that when your partner gets the opportunity to spend time with you he or she is shocked by the difference in your demeanor or character. Here is an important piece of advice when in a long-distance relationship: Just be you.

Why People Wear Masks

A long-distance relationship can start to feel like a game after a while. This happens because of the distance. You have your "normal" life, which includes your work, friends, and immediate surroundings. Then, on the other hand, you have a partner who is not part of your "normal" life because he or she is not around. Your partner might only appear in your life periodically, and when your partner shows up on your doorstep, it interrupts the normal flow of life you have. Even if you are happy to see them, it is a deviation from your typical routine.

Wearing a mask is a defense mechanism. Being in a long-distance relationship can be painful. You want to be able to hug your partner at the end of the day. You long to share everyday experiences with them. Many emotions can be present in a long-distance relationship, so emotional coping tools can pop up.

This does not mean that wearing a mask and presenting yourself as something other than who you are is healthy. To the contrary, this can be damaging to your relationship and can leave you feeling as though you are going through life playing too many roles. You will wind up feeling exhausted and wondering who you are. Although you might form these masks as simple coping mechanisms — and perhaps not even realize that you are doing so — your partner might regard it as deceptive. How would you feel if your partner was always sunny and positive when talking to you on the phone but completely gloomy the moment you were together in the same room?

The Split Personalities

The masks people create when they are in long-distance relationships are not the same as "split personalities" that are characteristic of Dissociative Identity Disorder, formerly known as "Multiple Personality Disorder." So, if you have found you have masks of your own, do not assume this means you need to rush off to a therapist for psychoanalysis. Just recognize that you have formed these masks, and you need to make an effort to present yourself as you truly are to your partner. Just be real.

Who are you?

You cannot expect your partner to know who you are if you are not even sure who you are. With a partner away, you may have time for self-reflection that will allow you to search your own feelings and desires and figure out who you are. Think about it this way: Are you who you want to be, or are you who you think people expect you to be?

If you and your partner have a solid relationship, there is a good chance that your partner still enjoys being with you even when you do not feel particularly cheerful, social or even polite. This is not to say that your partner happily should accept you yelling at him or her. Instead, it means that even on days when you cannot muster the energy to handle everything you usually handle, your partner is still just as in love with you as those days when you are on your "A-game." Partners in a flourishing long-distance relationship accept each other for who they really are, and they do not try to put on a show in an attempt to present a perfect image to one another.

Be you. The truth is that if you do not know who you are, then there is little chance of your long-distance relationship flourishing because you may not be presenting yourself to your partner in an authentic way. Figure out what you want your life to be, and not necessarily what your family or friends want your life to be. When you have figured this out, you then need to decide how your partner fits into the grand scheme of things when it comes to your life. Remember that discovering yourself and developing your personality does not automatically mean your relationship is doomed. You might both find that your relationship is strengthened by exploring who you truly want to be.

You with your partner

Do you change when you are with your partner? Whether you feel more at ease than usual or if you are exhausted from desperately trying to be perfect during the limited time you have together, you might feel as though you are not yourself when you spend time together. Initial awkwardness is common and expected among long-distance couples when they are able to have time together. If you spend that time feeling as though you are putting on an act then you have fallen into an unhealthy pattern of trying to be someone you are not. This is not good for you, your partner, or your relationship. *You will learn more about making the most of the time you have together in Chapter 8.*

People who are in long-distance relationships might feel pressure to present a perfect version of themselves during visits. Spending time with your partner face-to-face can be a rare treat for people in long-distance relationships, so it is easy to see how time together might be something you want to go well. You might fear that a bad visit might be the end of the relationship. After all, it can be hard work to make a long-distance relationship flourish, and face-to-face visits can be seen as the reward for all the hard work. If you do not have what you think is a perfect visit then you might worry that your partner will no longer want to put forth the effort to keep the two of you together.

However, there is no such thing as perfection in a relationship. There are going to be times when you are cranky, irritated, tired, sick, or just plain boring, and the same goes for your partner. People in traditional relationships deal with these things all the time because they are around their partners more frequently than those people in long-distance relationships. Everyone gets moody sometimes. These feelings are not invalid just because you're in a long-distance relationship. Honesty is the best policy. After all, if your partner was grouchy after a rough day at school, would you rather he or she told you up front that the grouchiness was a direct result of a tough day or have him or her pretend everything was fine when it was not?

When you have the opportunity to be with your partner face-to-face, be yourself. This does not mean to spend all your time together complaining about everything, but do not try to hide who you are. If your relationship has any hopes of overcoming the issues that come with long distance, make sure you are not putting on masks and pretending to be something you are not. If your partner truly cares about you, there should be no need for you to pretend. Give your partner the opportunity to fall in love with the real you.

You apart from your partner

It is quite typical to feel you are one person when you are with your partner and then feel different when chatting over the phone or on a computer. These varying forms of communication are so different it might prompt you to vary how you present yourself depending on which form of communication you are using at the time. Talking on the phone or chatting online is different from talking in the same room.

Some people present a different version of themselves in these conversations, particularly when it comes to avoiding any topics of possible conflict. Think about how easy it is to realize that something is troubling your partner when you are having a conversation face-to-face. Your partner might look away instead of looking you in the eye or might fidget his or her hands. On the other hand, when a conversation takes place over the phone or the computer, it is easier to mask tension.

It is normal to feel disconnected from your significant other when you are unable to have any time together. As a result, you might find yourself putting on an act when you do get the chance to chat with your partner, and you might not even realize you are doing it.

Phone and Internet conversations can also help people to cover up things. Masks are not necessarily unintentional. In instances when one partner is cheating on another, it can be harder to discover the issue when the main form of communication is not face-to-face. In this instance, the mask the cheating partner wears is intentional and fundamentally damaging to the relationship.

You with other people

Having a strong social circle can be of tremendous value when your partner is not around because you do not feel as isolated as you would if your life lacked social interaction. Problems can arise, however, when you are one person with your friends and another person with your partner. In this instance, you have the potential to ruin not only your romantic relationship, but also the relationships you have with your friends.

If you have the tendency to be one way with your friends and another way with your partner, do not be shocked when your friends react oddly at how you behave when your partner visits. You might be accused of acting like someone else or playing the role of a perfect partner. This situation will not help your partner and your friends connect because they might assume it is your partner's fault that you're acting weird. In this instance, it will only be a matter of time before someone pulls you aside and asks about your differing behavior.

There are those friends who bring out the goofy side of you, and there are those friends you act calmer with. It is natural (and normal) to adjust slightly to each person you interact with, but it becomes a different matter when your personality does a major shift when it comes to your group of friends versus your partner. It is an easy pattern to fall into. You might see your friends often, but do not get to see your partner as much. The trick is to try to present who you really are to your friends and your partner.

Avoiding Masks

It is difficult to wind up wearing masks if you are true to yourself consistently, but it can still occur. You might have an unconscious or even conscious desire to make sure your partner does not feel as though everything is changing while he or she is gone, so, if you stay exactly the same, then there will not be any problems.

This idea does not work because you are not a still being. You are constantly changing and evolving your identity, and your surroundings change as well. Suppose the next time you will see your partner is in six months, and then, think about all the changes that can occur in your life in half a year. What are the chances you will be exactly the same person you were when your partner left six months ago? You are bound to change, and there is no reason to mask these changes.

Once again, this is where communication is important in a long-distance relationship. You will find yourself wearing a mask with your partner if you censor yourself and do not share the changes going on in your life. Suppose you join swim team, start a club, or jump feet-first into your dream of running for student-body president while your partner is away? These things change people, and although the changes might be incredibly positive, big events in your life will change who you are and how you spend your days. These are the changes to convey to your partner. If not, your partner might feel left out and might panic because of all the changes he or she is missing.

That's So Awkward

If you initially met your partner face-to-face, having a long-distance relationship that survives with telephone and computer communication can feel awkward and forced. This is especially true if you do not care for these forms of communication, which is the case with many people. It is one thing to use the phone to order a pizza or to compose email intended for teachers, but it is another thing to try to convey your emotions using these methods.

Here are tips for making the most of the communication methods available to you:

- Picture your partner in front of you when you have a phone conversation. If it helps, look at a photo of your partner during the conversation, or close your eyes to block out everything else around you.

- Use Facetime, Skype or other video chat methods frequently. This allows you to see your partner while you chat, which removes some of the communication barriers that can come with long-distance relationships. If you feel awkward in front of the camera or distracted by your own face in the computer screen, turn off the feature that allows you to see yourself on the screen and just concentrate on the image of your partner.

- Compose email as though you are having a conversation with your partner. Avoid making the email sound like business or academic correspondence, which initially might be difficult for you if you spend time writing formal correspondence for work or school. Sometimes it helps to read email aloud before sending it. If it sounds forced or stuffy to you, there is a chance it will sound forced or stuffy to your partner.

- Tell your partner you feel awkward. Your partner would rather have you admit that you feel awkward chatting on the phone or over the Internet instead of you sounding uncomfortable but not explaining why.

- Accept that the forms of communication available to you might not be perfect, but they are certainly better than nothing. It was not long ago when couples had to rely solely on postal mail when away from each other. Now is a convenient time to be in a long-distance relationship because of all the communication methods available.

- Give yourself time to adjust. Even if you are not a big fan of talking over the phone, you might be pleasantly surprised eventually to find that you do not mind it, particularly when talking over the phone gives you the opportunity to chat with your partner.

When you feel awkward about talking on the phone or over the Internet, make sure not to put up a mask. You might choose your words too carefully, or you might not dive as deeply into the conversation as your partner would like. Do not allow your dislike for these forms of communication to lessen your personality or thoughts. If you want your relationship to thrive, you have to become used to using whatever forms of communication are available.

Chapter 4

Setting Goals

Setting goals is an important step to take in a long-distance relationship. Most people consider a long-distance arrangement a temporary one, with an eventual goal of being physically together at some point. If no definitive goals are set for the relationship, how can you know if you are heading in the right direction? If you and your partner work together to define what you want in your relationship then you can take proper steps to move the relationship toward your eventual goal.

When you are both in agreement about short-term and long-term goals, certain decisions become easier to make as a couple. When questions arise regarding topics such as college acceptance, it is important to ask, "How can we best solve this issue while still working toward our goals?" Setting goals can be an annoying task, especially if you are cautious about confronting your partner with a request for clarification on your relationship status. When it comes down to it, though, the point is to succeed in your long-distance relationship. Without clearly defined goals, it is difficult to flourish because you do not know what you are aiming for.

The Importance of Goals

Do not discount the importance of looking toward the future in your long-distance relationship. Although some couples try to avoid having a big talk about the future, when you are not physically near your partner, it becomes even more important to define clearly where you expect your relationship to wind up. So, although you initially might feel uncomfortable bringing up the big question of where the relationship is going, the question might help your relationship and allow it to thrive as you work toward your mutual goals.

Although important, you do not want to focus merely on your long-term goals. Short-term goals also need to be addressed. When is the next time the two of you will be together in the same room? How often do you want to have telephone conversations? How many texts per day do you need from your partner to feel you are getting the right of amount of attention?

Discussing your mutual goals means there are no big question marks in your relationship. If you know the two of you have the eventual goal of someday living together, the mutual decisions you make can lead toward that goal. If you know your partner expects you to call every night before going to bed, you will understand when your partner is sad when you forget to call. Your relationship goals clearly define your short-term and long-term directions, and when your relationship's direction is defined, it becomes easier to navigate.

The eventual goal of being together and someday shedding the label of "long-distance relationship" is one of the most important decisions you can make together. Without the goal of eventually eliminating this title, you and your partner will be left to wonder whether the long-distance arrangement is worth it.

Calm down

If reading about the importance of defining your relationship goals makes you feel anxious, take a deep breath, and realize that this is not something you have to do this minute. Your partner will be quite confused if you suddenly call him or her and demand to know where the relationship is going and when exactly the two of you can live in the same town. If your partner does not realize your sudden interrogation is coming from a desire to keep your relationship alive, he or she might feel suffocated and, perhaps, even panic.

Before talking to your partner about setting goals for your long-distance relationship, take a moment to pause, and ask yourself this question: What do you want? Do you like things the way they are, or are there changes you would like to see in your relationship? Do you have a deep desire someday to live with your partner, or does the thought of giving up the freedom your long-distance arrangement allows make you feel nervous? It is important to know what you want before you start asking your partner what he or she wants, otherwise you will not know if the two of you are in sync and moving toward the same goals.

Put simply; be prepared to know what you want in your relationship before you ask the same question to your partner. You do not have to have an answer carved in stone, but have an idea of what you want to hear from your partner before you even ask.

Quick Survival Tip

Do not feel selfish in examining what you want out of your relationship. You are entitled to know what you want and to make your desires clearly known to your partner. You will have a difficult time being on the same page as your partner if you do not accurately convey your ideas of what the relationship should look like now and down the road. Your partner cannot read your mind.

How to Set Goals

Setting goals does not have to be a huge endeavor. Think about the goals you set throughout your day already. You might have a goal of what time you will eat your lunch, what you will eat, and what time you will get back to whatever it was you were doing before you stopped to eat lunch. When you realize you set goals on a continual basis, the idea of setting goals for your long-distance relationship might not seem as daunting.

Keep in mind that these are not goals to set on your own, nor are they goals to keep to yourself. Although where you eat lunch does not affect your long-distance relationship, it certainly affects your relationship when you decide to make a goal of visiting your partner at least once a month. What if it is not feasible for your partner to visit you every month? There might be financial constraints or schedule problems that make it impossible to meet the goal of monthly visits. If you set this goal in your mind, yet neglect to pass this expectation along to your partner, your relationship might encounter difficulties when you find your goal is not working. This is an instance where goal setting should be paired with open communication to avoid frustration for everyone involved.

To get started in setting goals, here are questions to consider:

- Where do you expect your relationship to go?

- Where do you think your partner expects your relationship to go?

- What would be the ideal situation for your relationship in a few months? A year from now? Five years from now?

- What changes need to be made before you can accomplish your goals?

You already might have covered these questions with your partner. However, it is still a good idea to explore the other possible goals the two of you might have, while also discussing personal goals that might only initially pertain to one of you but eventually will affect you both. For example, suppose you always have assumed you would go to an out-of-state college. This goal should be discussed with your partner, especially if the two of you have never discussed it before. What if your partner has no idea your plan is to go to an out-of-state school? It is better to have this conversation earlier as opposed to later.

Here are tips to help you determine your goals, as an individual and as a couple:

- Examine your personal goals and the goals you have for your relationship and consider your partner's goals .

- Think about long-term and short-term goals and eliminate any that are not feasible.

- Compose a list of the goals that are directly or indirectly related to your long-distance relationship's success.

- Once you both agree that your goals are important, you now have a tangible list of goals that will help guide future decisions about your relationship.

Keep in mind that goals certainly can change. You do not want to fall into the trap of thinking your list of goals is the be-all and end-all guideline for every decision you make as a couple. Instead, consider the list of goals to be what is right for you now, and agree that a time might come when you will have to be flexible about where your relationship is heading. After all, you do not want to pass up an extraordinary opportunity or not get to attend your dream school just because these unexpected opportunities were not listed on your goal list. Take life as it comes, and use your goal list as a guide, but with the understanding that goals can change frequently. The important thing is to agree mutually on your relationship goals.

Putting Plans in Motion

You have your list of goals for the long term and the short term. Now an important step for putting your plans into motion is figuring out how to concentrate on your goals. As was the case with composing your original list, this is not something to do on your own and then expect your partner to come along for the ride. Concentrating on your goals is something that should be done together, and each goal should get the seal of approval from both people involved.

Figure out which goals are most important to you and to your partner while also examining which goals will best serve to strengthen your relationship. For example, if you both agree that having monthly visits with each other is more important than saving up for a large expense later on, such as buying a home together or having an elaborate wedding, then the goal of monthly visits will be more important than your long-term goal with a major expense. It will become apparent as you find that many of your goals are related in one way or another; at the least, you will find you have to wait on some of your goals to make the other goals happen.

Try to be realistic when prioritizing your goals. Look at the possible repercussions associated with your goals, especially emotional and financial. A goal of visiting your partner each month might be incredibly beneficial to your emotional connection, but the financial impact might be too much for your checkbook to handle. So, although it is good to see each other once a month to feel emotionally connected, your relationship might start to suffer when you find that the frequent travel expenses are too expensive. Being in love is good, but being overdrawn on your bank account and delinquent on your credit card bill is enough to put a damper on any relationship. Do not allow romance to override practicality because this, inevitably, will lead to a relationship you cannot maintain.

When priorities differ

You might find that your priorities are different from those of your partner, and with some couples, this can be a problem. Suppose you and your partner spend time composing lists of long-term goals and then comparing them over the phone only to find that your No. 1 goal going to an out-of-state college differs from your partner's goal of becoming a professional athlete. When you discover the two of you do not necessarily have the same goals to work toward, this can be difficult.

You already know that communication in a long-distance relationship is important. If you discover you and your partner have different goals, take this as an opportunity to discuss what your goals should be together, and do not automatically assume your differing goals are a solid indication that your relationship is doomed. If the two of you can talk about your main priorities openly without allowing the discussion to turn into an argument, you might find that your goals can work quite well together. Having mutual goals that have been discussed thoroughly can make for a solid foundation for a couple, particularly when they are in a long-distance relationship. When you have solid goals you are both working toward, you still connected despite being physically apart. This can strengthen your relationship.

Quick Survival Tip

Red flags should go off in your head if your long-term, long-distance partner refuses to discuss setting plans in motion so the two of you can live closer to one another, especially if you and your partner see each other infrequently. Some people cling to a long-distance relationship because they do not want to make a commitment. If you find yourself in this situation, examine whether this relationship actually has the chance to flourish or if your partner is set on keeping the relationship stagnant forever.

Not all differing goals can be melded together so cohesively. Should you leave your partner and try to find someone who has the same goals as you? *You will learn more about deciding to call it quits in Chapter 10.* However, for now, do not assume that differing goals mean the relationship must come to a screeching halt.

Your goal list is more of an outline than a permanent schedule for how the future of your relationship will go. Just because your partner does not list the same goals as you now does not mean they will not appear on the list in the future. Use the tools for communication you have to openly express how you feel about the differences on your lists of goals. If you allow your mind to make illogical, cognitive leaps, such as "He did not list moving in together on his list. He must not want to move in with me. This relationship is doomed," then your relationship certainly will suffer. Instead, be truthful and open with your partner about your concerns. Tell your partner you are surprised to not see moving in together (or whatever your goal is) on his or her list, share that this goal is at the top of your list, and invite an honest discussion about the differences between the lists. Do not hurl accusations or be hurt by anything that appears on your partner's list, and listen carefully to what your partner has to say about his or her goals. One of the worst things you can do is to not listen and instead, formulate your response in your head while waiting for your turn to talk. This will not result in a productive discussion.

You might not be able to have this discussion with your partner face-to-face, but the same rules apply. Keep in mind what you have learned about telephone and email communications, and when you need clarification about something, ask for it instead of just assuming that you understand the intended meaning to be something insulting. When an important discussion about your goals has to take place and when there are differences that must be discussed, it can be incredibly difficult to be long distance because it lessens the speed and effectiveness of communication. You are talking about short-term and long-term goals, and when it comes down to it, there is no rush to get everything solved right this moment. Give it time.

Understanding Exclusivity

You might be wondering why a discussion about exclusivity is in a chapter about setting relationship goals. The answer is simple: Your list of shared goals will fall under the assumed umbrella of exclusivity to each other, and if both partners are not on board with being exclusive, the rest of the goals might fall apart.

If you are in a long-distance relationship where exclusivity has not been discussed or even assumed, then you might want to put the brakes on any discussion about your mutual goals until the two of you can figure out the status of your relationship. Do you want to discuss moving in or going to college with someone who is still dating other people?

For your long-distance relationship to succeed, the two of you might want to be exclusive with each other. Being in a long-distance relationship can be difficult, but it is worth it if you know there is the potential for a future between the two of you. Putting effort into a relationship when you do not even know if your partner is fully on board with being your partner is not much of a relationship. If you are going to take the plunge and say the two of you are involved in a long-distance relationship — and you both want the relationship to work — it should be stated clearly that this relationship is exclusive and that you are committed to each other. This means no dates with other people and no online flirtations with other people, and there should be a shared list of goals between the two of you about where your relationship eventually will go.

This can be a tricky discussion if it has not yet occurred naturally. The truth is that if you have not heard the words from your partner that the two of you are exclusive with each other, you might find that your partner does not realize the two of you are not supposed to date other people. It might seem like a cop-out when your partner thinks, "How was I supposed to know that I am not allowed to hang out with people?" But this is how some minds work. For some people, exclusivity has to be spelled out. Decide what exclusivity means to you, find out what it means to your partner, and make sure you are on the same page. For you, exclusivity might allow you to hang out with anyone you please, but to your partner, exclusivity might mean you shouldn't even get a meal with anyone other than them. It is not enough to say, "We are exclusive" in a long-distance relationship. The two of you should be able to say, "We are exclusive, and this is what being exclusive means to us."

Exclusivity is one of the most important decisions the two of you can make when trying to make your long-distance relationship flourish. If you are going to put this much effort into a relationship, the payoff should be that you know your partner is putting at least as much effort into the relationship as you are. If you do not have an exclusive relationship, it becomes too easy to stray and lose sight of your mutual goals as a couple. If you want your relationship to thrive, exclusivity is a decision that has to be made together.

Avoid the Cheating Trap

When you are in a long-distance relationship, the threat of one of you straying from the relationship is real and potentially heightened by the fact that the two of you cannot monitor each other's activities like you could if you lived under the same roof. This is certainly not to say that everyone is just waiting for the opportunity to cheat on his or her partner; most people do not set out to do so. For many people who wind up cheating, it starts out innocently but then turns into something else entirely.

You and your partner need to be clear about the expectations you set for each other when it comes to other people. You cannot blow up at your partner for having lunch with a friend who fits their "type" if the two of you have not clearly stated that one-on-one lunches are off limits. Talk to each other about expectations and perceptions. Your partner might not think he or she is doing anything wrong when going over to a friend's house for a movie night, but when that friend is questionable and the movie night goes late into the evening with no one else present, your perception of the situation might be different than the perception of your partner. You see it as an opportunity for your partner's friend to make a move while your partner sees it as an opportunity to see a movie with a friend.

If you and your partner have clear expectations set for each other about interactions with others, it becomes difficult to argue about what is "right" and what is "wrong." Instead, you rely on what your partner has told you about his or her comfort level with what you do, and in turn, you have revealed what you find acceptable. If you have not yet had this discussion with your partner, start with these questions:

- What is unacceptable behavior with someone who is "just a friend?"

- Are one-on-one interactions with people of your partner's "type" allowed? Does this change if it is related to school?

- Is it all right to text friends of that are your partner's "type?"

There are no right or wrong answers to these questions. The "right" answer to these and related questions are the answers that you and your partner agree on. It is incredibly important to set guidelines with your partner when you are away from each other. This is not an area you want to remain vague on your mutual expectations for behavior. You might assume that your partner has the same expectations as you on this topic, but unless the two of you talk it through, you might be surprised to find your partner has been engaging in activities that you find unacceptable even if they are not classified as "cheating." How would you feel if your partner worked in the same room as a friend of they may see as attractive but then rationalized it by saying they were working together on a project? Your partner might see this as nothing more than doing homework, but you might see it as grounds for breaking up. Perception should be a huge part of figuring out what is acceptable for you and for your partner.

You cannot control what your partner does while away from you, but you can take responsibility for your own actions and not fall into the cheating trap. Even if you do not realize it, someone might view your long-distance situation as an opportunity to swoop in and give you the emotional attention you cannot get from your partner. You might appear to be needy or vulnerable, even if you do not portray neediness or vulnerability. It is enough that your partner is miles away.

Beware of friends who appear eager to be your sounding board, or worse yet, who say things along the lines of, "If your partner loved you, he/she would be here right now" or "What your partner does not know will not harm him/her." Be on the lookout for people who seem excessively affectionate. It is one thing for a genuine friend to give you a big hug, but it is another thing entirely for a friend to hold a hug for longer than what would be considered reasonable among friends. Listen to the voice inside your head. If your internal voice starts saying your friend is making a move on you, there is a chance you are right.

Continuing to play the flirting game with someone who is attracted to you is extremely risky. It might feel incredible to have someone pay attention to you and make you feel appreciated, but when it comes down to it, you have to decide if you want to be committed to your partner or if you want something else. Trust is one of the most important factors in a successful long-distance relationship, and if you are doing things that betray your partner's trust — whether he or she finds out or not — it is completely damaging to your relationship.

Surround yourself with people who care about you, but remove yourself from the presence of people who want more from you. If you get the feeling one of your friends might have feelings for you beyond friendship, use caution, and do not allow yourself to get into a situation in which something might happen. It can be different for people in long-distance relationships. You may not realize how severely you miss affection. Unfortunately, there are people who will prey on you and know you might feel deprived of attention. Do not allow people to take advantage of you and, consequently, to ruin the trust your partner has in you.

Being in a long-distance relationship is an adult decision that takes effort. You made the decision to be with your partner despite the miles, so you also must make the decision not to allow yourself in a situation where your behavior is a contradiction to your decision to be with your partner.

One piece of advice about cheating while in a long-distance relationship: There is a saying that originated from a Bible verse that says what happens in the dark will come to light. Do not think that just because you are miles away from your partner, he or she will not find out if you cheat. In today's world of constant monitoring, social networks, and fast information sharing, a quick lapse of judgment can be the talk of your social group in minutes. That means a single kiss you share with a friend can be common knowledge before you even make it home from your friend's house.

Be Great Solo and Together

You might feel as though you have two different lives when you are in a long-distance relationship: the life on your own and the life with your partner. When your partner is not around, it can be difficult to integrate your two lives. It is important to pay attention to both lives and to work toward being great with and without your partner.

Why is this important? If you are miserable in your solo life (you hate school, you do not have friends, you spend time bored out of your mind), your relationship with your partner will suffer as well. You need to be happy with yourself and your own life before you can hope to be happy with someone else. The reality of a long-distance relationship is that your partner cannot be there all the time. You need to be able to rely on yourself and have fun, so you do not feel as lonely when your partner cannot be there for you.

Avoid the Pity Party

Being in a long-distance relationship can stink. Some days you just want to hang out with your partner, tell him or her about your day and forget your stress.

These relationships can be incredibly hard, and sometimes it might seem like nobody in the world understands what you go through. That being said, you made the decision with your partner to stay together despite the distance, and when it comes down to it, being with your partner is worth it even if there are miles between the two of you. Here is the key: Acknowledge that what you are doing is tough, but keep in mind the reasoning behind what you are doing. Your partner is the person you want to be with. Staying together in a long-distance relationship will be one of the hardest things you deal with in your relationship, but in the future, you might look back on it as completely worth the effort.

Several problems arise when you indulge in a pity party about your current situation. You might become bitter about the distance, which certainly will have an effect on how you deal with your partner. Your negativity can be infectious, so the next thing you know, you might find yourself dealing with a partner who has fallen into his or her own pity party. Your relationship is going to have a difficult time thriving if the two of you are too busy feeling sorry for yourselves to interact with each other as a couple. You cannot expend the necessary energy to take care of yourself and the emotional needs of your partner if you fall too deeply into a woe-is-me pattern of thinking.

Acknowledge that a long-distance relationship is the result of a choice you made. Consider what compelled you to make that decision in the first place. When it comes down to it, you are not a victim of circumstance, but instead, you are a person who wants to stay with your partner and are willing to endure inconveniences to make it happen. It is terribly romantic when you stop to think about it, and if you can find a way to keep a positive spin on what you are going through, it will help you stay positive and keep everything in perspective.

Again, keep open communication with your partner. If you are frustrated by your circumstances, talk to your partner about your feelings. Just make sure that you do not attack your partner emotionally or complain to him or her all the time. Present your feelings, do not throw any blame in your partner's direction, and then listen to what your partner has to say. You might find that your partner feels similarly, and once you realize that being in a long-distance relationship is not easy on either one of you, it might become apparent that your partner is willing to sacrifice for you just as you are willing to sacrifice for him or her. Two people willing to sacrifice for each other is a recipe for success when it comes to just about any relationship, but it is especially true for long-distance relationships.

Tips for Enjoying Solo Time

Just because your partner is miles away does not mean you have to avoid having fun on your own. Having a satisfyingly busy life can translate into feeling more fulfilled even though your partner is away. Find things you enjoy doing, and spend time with positive people who understand what you are going through with your partner away.

Here are tips for making sure you enjoy your own life while you are away from your partner:

- Grant yourself permission to have fun even though your partner cannot join in the fun. A happier you will lead to a better relationship with your partner. If your partner has issues with you going out and having innocent fun then you need to have a discussion with your partner about trust and compromise.

- Find activities that can be done with friends, but also find some activities which are meant to be done alone. Watching movies, reading books, joining a sports team, and riding bikes are a few examples of the activities you can do that are fun and will not be full of happy couples that remind you how much you miss your partner.

- Consider using the time away from your partner to try some new hobbies or activities that you have wanted to try but have not had the opportunity to do. If you have wanted to train for a race, spend afternoons running. If you want to take up guitar, set a practice schedule that will allow you to be in the habit of learning before your partner returns. Think less of your time away as something you must get through and more as an opportunity to focus on yourself for a while.

- Commit some of your solo time to your relationship. What can you do in your spare time to make your relationship grow? Whether it is writing letters to your partner, scheduling a flower delivery for your partner's birthday, or learning to bake your partner's favorite dessert, you can do things that will give you a sense of accomplishment and help your relationship thrive. When you do these things, it says to your partner, "I care enough about you to take time out of my free time to make you feel loved."

Even though you miss your boyfriend or girlfriend, you still can enjoy life while you are away from each other. As long as you are doing things that will not harm your relationship, being active and content will be better for you and your partner. Wallowing in sadness because you are in a long-distance relationship is not going to do you or your partner any favors. Life does not pause because you and your partner are not physically together. Instead of spending your time waiting for your next visit with your partner, get on with your life and enjoy yourself. When you can enjoy your day-to-day life, you will be able to deal with the stresses of a long-distance relationship and will rely less on your partner as your source of happiness.

Take Care of You and Your Relationship

Keeping a long-distance relationship alive can take effort, and there is a chance your stress levels increase. It can be easier to deal with the extra stress if you are making an effort to take care of yourself. You also will find that your long-distance relationship will flourish if you put effort into taking care of your relationship as much as you put effort into taking care of yourself. It might sound like significant work and effort, but taking care of yourself and your relationship will be worth it in the end.

Taking care of you

When you get plenty of rest, eat right, and get enough exercise, you feel better altogether, even if you are not in a long-distance relationship. Taking care of yourself allows you to be the best you can be.

Your emotions

Some people lose themselves when they get into a relationship. When the relationship is a long-distance one, it can be a confusing time. It is common to experience a bit of sadness occasionally during this time. You might feel jealous, which displays itself as sadness when you see other happy couples enjoying each other's company. You might find yourself feeling lonely when you know other people are spending time with their loved ones, and you are not able to be physically near your partner. You need to monitor your emotions constantly while you are in a long-distance relationship.

If you feel depressed, try to pinpoint from where that particular feeling is coming. If you find yourself feeling gloomy, do not just dismiss the feelings as "feeling blue," and then ignore the sadness. Instead, figure out where the gloominess is coming from and what you can do about it.

This might sound easier said than done, but with practice, you can teach yourself to be in touch with your feelings, so you do not fall into the trap of sulking in negative emotions. The trick is to analyze your negative emotions the moment they arise. You do not have to be a trained professional to do this, but you do have to be willing to be honest with yourself about how you feel.

Here is how it works: When you realize you are experiencing a negative emotion, such as sadness, anger, or frustration, take a mental step back, and figure out why you are experiencing those feelings. Instead of "I'm just having a bad day today," it should be more along the lines of, "I am frustrated because I missed a call from my partner last night, and this frustration is putting me in a tense mood." The power behind recognizing the root of your emotions is that it helps you stop the negative behavior and then try to turn your emotions around. If you can recognize that your tense mood is a direct result of frustration stemming from having missed your partner's phone call the previous night, remind yourself there will be more phone calls from your partner in the future. Your partner probably would not approve of your spending the day in a frustrated mood because you missed a call.

What is the result of this emotional self-analysis? Think about the previous example. Suppose your partner calls, and the first thing you say to him or her is, "I missed your call last night, and today has just been the worst day ever." You are putting the blame on your partner when he or she wanted to chat and just happened to call at a time when you were unavailable. Do this enough and there is a chance your partner will start to associate calling you with the potential for a bad experience. Your partner might not even realize that he or she has made this association subconsciously. All your partner will know is that he or she does not feel like calling you anymore.

Now take the same situation, but instead, you say to your partner, "I am sorry I missed your call last night. I was sad that I missed your call, but I am happy to talk to you now." These words change everything dramatically. By telling your partner you were sad to miss the call, but not making it sound like there were major negative repercussions for the missed call, you encourage your partner to keep calling because he or she knows what the phone calls mean to you. When you tell your partner how happy you are to talk to him or her, you set the tone for the rest of the conversation.

It is unlikely that you can take a step back from every emotion and analyze what you are feeling, especially when there are intense emotions involved. On the other hand, if you acknowledge negative feelings and try to figure out a rational way to view those emotions, you become a better communicator with your partner. You might even become a nicer person to deal with.

What if you just cannot seem to grasp the idea of taking control of your emotions, and you frequently find yourself in a deep depression or fits of rage? When your negative emotions start to have a negative impact on your life, it might be time to seek professional help. Give yourself permission to get the help you need so you can take control of your emotional life. A licensed therapist can give you the coping tools you need to not allow this stressful time in your life to define who you are forever.

Your physical health

Studies point to physical health having a positive impact on emotional well-being. One medical study from the University of Arizona states that there is a direct correlation between exercise and positive mental health. The Mayo Clinic also reveals that people who make time to take care of themselves and include physical activity in their regular routines may experience better moods because of the increased production of chemicals in the brain directly related to mood regulation. This is certainly not to say that people who are fit are always happy, no that people who are not fit spend their days in grief. Instead, the idea is that physical activity enhances your life in a variety of ways, and one of the benefits can be emotional well-being.

The goal is to take care of your relationship and take care of yourself. This is not a selfish goal. Instead, it is an acknowledgement that you can give more to your partner when you have invested in yourself. Taking time out every day, or a few times a week, so you can take a walk or visit the gym can help you in a wide range of ways. You can make your health better and find that you deal with stress better. Your emotional responses will be more reasonable than they might have otherwise been.

If you are already fit, make sure you stay on course and do not allow your relationship's long-distance arrangement change your progress. If you are frequently able to travel to see your partner, try not to fall into the trap of gaining weight when you travel. It can be easy not to pay attention to your caloric intake when you are away from home. These trips to see your partner might feel like mini-vacations where you do not have to worry about what you eat. The problem is when these mini-vacations are frequent because the damage done during these trips can add up.

If you are not fit, consider using this time away from your partner as an excellent opportunity to take control of your health. Start small with daily walks after dinner, or start exercising at home. If joining a gym is financially feasible, find a gym close to home or work and try to attend group fitness classes or even spend time with a personal trainer. It does not take long to see results when you dedicate time to getting in shape, especially if you are dedicated to the process.

There is more than one reason to get serious about your physical health, but when it comes right down to it, taking care of yourself is one of the important things you can do in a long-distance relationship to ensure you are at your best. It is easier to deal with the stresses of having a partner who is not physically around if you get regular exercise and eat right.

CASE STUDY: EXPERT ADVICE

Dr. Amber Tyler

Chronic stress is actually very hard on the body. Aside from the emotional effects people typically think of such as anxiety, depression and sleep problems, a whole host of physical symptoms can occur. Chronic stress can raise your blood pressure. It increases your risk for heart disease and diabetes. It can affect digestion, causing acid reflux (heartburn), constipation or diarrhea. When you are under a lot of stress, your muscles tend to be tenser, which triggers headaches and muscular pains such as back pain, shoulder pain, etc. Stress increases the likelihood that you will clench or grind your teeth in your sleep, which causes problems with your jaw and can lead to broken teeth. People who are under chronic stress generally experience an overall higher level of pain.

Stress triggers a "fight or flight" response, which is very beneficial for sudden stressful situations such as an attack on your safety or a tornado, but not very beneficial as a perpetual condition. When you experience chronic stress, your body lives in the "fight or flight" response all the time, though to a lesser degree than in sudden intense situations. This means that your body is making and circulating increased levels of stress hormones, especially cortisol. This has a lot of impact on the body. It impacts the immune system, making you more vulnerable to illness. It can contribute to cravings for sugary and fatty foods (comfort foods) and increases the conversion of things we eat into stored fat, so you gain weight.

The good news is that even if you cannot remove or change the source of your chronic stress, you can do something to counteract the effects. Exercise is the best medicine available for many health conditions, but especially for people under stress. Exercise increases your body's production of endorphins, a "feel good" chemical. Endorphins reduce symptoms associated with anxiety and depression, decrease pain levels, and boost your immune system. Exercise lowers your blood pressure, improves your body's processing of sugars (decreasing the risk of diabetes), and lowers cholesterol. People who exercise regularly fall asleep faster and sleep better than those who do not exercise. Exercise also helps people attain and maintain a healthy weight, which makes everyone feel better physically and emotionally.

There are so many ways to exercise that everyone should be able to find something. It can range from the traditional running or aerobics classes to something like a dance game on the Nintendo® Wii™ or Xbox® Kinect™ (Those games can burn a lot of calories). If you can afford it, joining a gym and consulting with a trainer can be useful because you are accountable to someone, and you want to get your money's worth. Take a martial arts class, yoga, pole dancing — whatever you can find that you will enjoy. If you can find a friend to do it with you, you will be more likely to continue because they can get you going on days you may have otherwise talked yourself out of working out. Then, you need to set goals, and they need to be reasonable goals. Do not start running with plans of training for a marathon. That is overwhelming, and it is easy to get discouraged and quit. A better goal in the beginning is something like exercising for 15 to 20 minutes three times a week. That is much more manageable. Once you have turned that goal into a habit, set a new goal, something like 30 minutes of exercise, five times a week. Gradually increase until you get where you want to be.

If you have a chronic health problem such as high blood pressure, heart disease, or a joint disorder, you should see your doctor before beginning an exercise program to determine what is the safest and most effective way for you to exercise. Very few people cannot exercise in some way. If you are otherwise healthy, then the most important first step is to find something you think is fun. If you do not like what you are doing, it is unlikely that you will stick with it.

Your relationship's health

You already know how important it is to take care of your emotional and physical health so that you can give your best self to your partner. You also need to realize that your relationship needs to be cultivated and cared for too. Just as you care for yourself because you know it is important, concentrate effort into taking care of your relationship.

This is different from taking care of your partner. Try to visualize your relationship as a separate entity. Your relationship is not necessarily a living, breathing thing. It is something, however, that needs attention and can easily fade away if it is not given sufficient attention. Couples who have traditional relationships can fall into an easy pattern of cultivating their relationships without even realizing they are doing so, but when you are in a long-distance relationship, it can take concerted effort.

Start by asking yourself this question: "How can I improve the health of my relationship with my partner?" You might already know you can do one thing to make your partner feel better about the relationship and another thing to make you feel better about the relationship. What can you do that will benefit both of you, thereby contributing to the health of the relationship?

Here is an example: Suppose you have the opportunity to go to an away game for school, which is the same school as your boyfriend's best friend. You have never met his best friend, and as far as you are concerned, it would be an awkward meeting, especially considering your boyfriend would not be present. Your partner tells you it is up to you whether you meet with his friend, so there is no pressure from him regarding what decision to make. When you examine the situation from an outside perspective, however, you realize that meeting your partner's best friend would strengthen your relationship for more than one reason. Your boyfriend might take it as a compliment that you took the time to meet him or her. The friend might take it as a sign of respect that you put time aside from your schedule to meet him. The decision to meet with your boyfriend's friend would benefit the relationship. This was not a decision you made because your partner urged you to or because you had a burning desire to meet your partner's best friend, but instead, you made the decision because you knew it would be best for your relationship as a whole.

You will encounter a wide variety of situations in which you have to decide what is best for your relationship when there is no clear benefit or drawback for you or your partner. When faced with these types of scenarios, ask yourself if there is a benefit to your relationship as a whole. Along those same lines, when faced with a decision that might have negative consequences to your relationship, think twice before going ahead.

Communication, paired with decision-making, that always looks toward the best interests of the relationship, will help your long-distance relationship grow.

Support from Others

Consider yourself fortunate if you have a large network of friends and family who are available to support you. People in long-distance relationships often feel isolated socially because they are not able to enjoy the same day-to-day interactions with partners that people in traditional relationships enjoy. If you have friends who make sure you still enjoy going out and having fun in a social setting, this can help you keep off feelings of being alone while your partner is miles away.

On the other hand, it is a delicate balance. You do not want to rely on other people so much that you start to become needy. You also do not want to fall into a pattern of turning to other people to fulfill you emotionally. Even if your partner is several time zones away, he or she should still be the one person who most fulfills you emotionally.

Family and close friends should offer you support and socialization. They should encourage you to still get out and have fun, but they should not encourage you to do things that would sabotage your relationship. It should be understood among all your friends and family that you are in a committed relationship, and just because you and your partner are not physically together does not mean you are available. Make sure you surround yourself with people who are on board with your relationship and who will not speak badly about your partner or your situation. It can be difficult to be in a long-distance relationship if the people around you are not supportive of the arrangement. If you listen to enough negative talk from people close to you, it might start to sound like the truth.

Your boyfriend or girlfriend should be your primary source of emotional support. This can be easier said than done when you are in a long-distance relationship, but as long as you keep the lines of communication open and accurately portray your need for emotional support to your partner, then it can be done. Keep in mind the old saying, "absence makes the heart grow fonder." Absence or distance does not compel people to stop caring about their partner's emotional needs. If your partner stops caring about your emotional needs just because there are miles separating the two of you, then there are bigger problems that need to be addressed.

Chapter 6

The Long-Distance Date

Just because you and your partner are not physically together does not mean that you cannot commit time to each other. The concept of a date — long-distance or otherwise — is to get time together and concentrate effort on staying connected. Although this preferably is done while physically together, a date certainly can occur long distance.

Now is a convenient time to be in a long-distance relationship. As long as you have the technological capabilities and know how to pull it off, you can have dates with your partner who is miles away but still feel like the two of you are in the same room. That is the beauty of video chat and similar technology. You can see your partner and see his or her surroundings while he or she can see your surroundings. There does not have to be any mystery about where your partner is calling you from or what coffee shop you are sitting in because with video, your partner can see everything that is surrounds you. This certainly can help the two of you feel more connected.

Even if you do not have the ability to use video or similar technology, other options are available. The point is to make a effort to spend time together when your attention is not on something else. This is a time when the two of you concentrate on each other and try to connect as best as you can, even while apart.

Not an Impossible Feat

Having a date with your partner who is away from you is possible, even though it might seem cheesy or awkward at times. To say, "I have a date with my boyfriend" and then sit down in front of a laptop's webcam at your kitchen table can feel odd, but once you get used to this method of "dating," you will soon find that these sessions can help the two of you feel closer. It is nice to know your girlfriend will drop everything else and clear her schedule to spend time with you — even if that time is not physically together, it can help strengthen the bond between the two of you.

Figure out what works best for your relationship. Is there a specific day and time that will work every week, or do your schedules make it impossible to know from one week to the next when you can spend virtual time together? Set a start time and end time for your date. You can adjust the end time of your date if the two of you are having a discussion or are enjoying each other's company too much to stop, but when two people live in different cities it is common for them both to have separate schedules and obligations. An end time for the date makes the entire process less daunting. A busy partner does not have to worry that the virtual date will drag on, particularly if there is still work to be done or if the time difference forces the date to happen late at night for one person.

Commit to a certain number of dates per week or month, if possible. This might be difficult for couples who have busy schedules or who cannot plan ahead because of other obligations, but if it works out to have a preset time and day for your date then it is something you can look forward to and anticipate. Do not feel pressure to entertain your partner on your dates. This is simply a time to dedicate to each other and to hang out — as much as two people can "hang out" when miles away from each other.

If you are intentional about setting time aside for your date, no matter how often or what form your date takes, this will help keep the two of you connected while also keeping the lines of communication open. For a long-distance relationship, these benefits are gold.

Date versus chat

There is a difference between an everyday chat on the phone or computer with your partner and a date to chat on the phone or computer. The difference is that a date is intentional. The time has been set aside, and it is understood that this specific time is intended for the two of you to spend time together. When you just happen to reach your partner to say hello, you might call or text at a time when your partner is not able to give you exclusive attention or when your partner is trying to get something else done. When a date has been set, you both know the focus should be solely on your partner and the things you want to talk about. When the conversation is a date, it takes precedence over everything else at that time.

These dates can be precious. When you are in a long-distance relationship, you can lose sight of why you allow yourself to be in this situation. You might wonder if the relationship is truly worth the extra effort. When your partner is willing — and perhaps even eager — to set time aside to spend time talking with you, it helps to remind you of how special your relationship is.

This is not to say that impromptu conversations are not of value, but there is also value in scheduling time together. Think of it this way: If the two of you lived in the same town and saw each other every day, you would still make plans to go out on dates together. There is something about setting time aside to be together that makes it special. You do not have to plan to do spectacular things on your date, just plan to be together.

Types of Dates

The types of dates you manage to have with your partner long-distance are more plentiful than you might realize. As long as you both have telephone and Internet capabilities, you might find that you can even vary the dating methods you try. This can be beneficial particularly if one or both or you do not feel comfortable with talking on the phone or chatting online because it allows you to explore different methods and decide which one works best for you.

Start out by designating a certain time and day for your date. Make sure it is a time and day when there are few or no distractions. Depending on where you are both located, you might want to vary the location that each of you goes to for the date. For example, both of you going to a coffee shop in your respective cities and talking to each other via phone or computer can make you feel less apart.

The telephone date

Make sure the details are out of the way before your telephone date. You want to ensure that a day and time has been set and that your phone is fully charged. Decide beforehand who will call whom, so there is no confusion. One of the biggest points of a phone date is to help your long-distance partner feel as though he or she has your undivided attention for a time.

What should you talk about on your phone date? Try to avoid the mundane things that get inserted into everyday conversation. This is not the time to talk about how your backpack broke or how your coach is driving you crazy. Talk about things that will help the two of you feel better connected, such as reasons why you love each other, what your plans are for the future together, or anything else that is a mutual topic that both of you easily can participate in chatting about.

Some long-distance couples get a kick out of sharing experiences throughout the week and then talking about them on phone dates. For example, reading the same book at the same pace, such as a chapter a night, and then discussing the book over the phone can help keep the two of you connected. This does not have to be a relationship book that the two of you read but, instead, can be anything that appeals to both of you. Find something that will hold your attention and the attention of your partner. You do not want to force a book on your partner that he or she will resent having to read, especially something along the lines of a self-help book if your partner does not feel the need to self-improve and sees the command to read the book as a dig.

Watching favorite TV shows or a movie together on a phone date can be fun, too. This is easy if you live in similar time zones or if you have the capability to access shows in other ways, such as on Netflix or on DVDs. For couples that share an interest in a certain show, this is a way to feel closer. Miles might separate the two of you, but you can still have shared experiences.

 Quick Survival Tip

Find out what your family's phone plan is. Long-distance relationships can result in significant time spent chatting on the phone, so it helps if you know how many minutes you have in a given month. Otherwise, long phone conversations can lead to a ridiculously huge phone bill at the end of the month.

The Video date

The Internet offers options for virtual dates with your partner. Whether you want to chat with your partner via Facetime or Skype with your partner for your date, the conversations happen in real time and can happen anywhere you have an Internet connection.

Skype is one of the best bets for a long-distance date, but it is not foolproof. If one or both of you have slow Internet connections, the chat might be more frustrating than anything else because the screen can slow down or freeze, and the sound quality can become distorted. The norm, however, is that the video is fine, and the quality of the picture and sound makes the conversation pleasant.

After the two of you have decided on a day and time, figure out the logistics beforehand, just as you would for a telephone date.

Are the two of you going to set up your laptops in specified places, such as at home or coffee shops? Make sure that wherever you set up, you have a connection to the Internet. Depending on the cell phones you and your partner have, you might be able to use the video chat on your phones. You might find that your laptop is the best bet for video chat, but again, this depends on the technology at your disposal.

If you plan to use Skype or a similar program, install this program ahead of time, and test it before the day your online date arrives. If your partner logs on to chat with you, and you do not show up online until 20 minutes later because you were downloading the program, he or she might wonder how committed to the process you are if you did not think to download the program beforehand.

If you are going to be in full sight of your partner because you are using a webcam for your Internet date, take time to spruce yourself up beforehand just as you would with a face-to-face date. Also, pay attention to your surroundings. No matter how much you dress yourself up before sitting down in front of the computer, if you are sitting in a messy room because you have not bothered to clean it, this is going to distract from the quality of the conversation. Remove anything in the webcam's view that might distract your partner. For example, if the two of you love a particular restaurant, but this restaurant is not available where your partner is, do not sit in front of the webcam slurping on a to-go cup from that restaurant. Your goal for your Internet date is to feel connected to your partner, not to remind your partner about the distance between the two of you.

This should go without saying, but it is important and needs to be mentioned: Your video date is not an appropriate time to have friends pop up and wave at your partner. Your partner might view this as a threat. Imagine chatting with your partner online and suddenly someone else shows up on the video, smiling and waving at you but with one arm around your partner. No matter how innocently this is intended, there is a chance that damage can be done. Your partner should walk away from the conversation feeling closer to you instead of walking away from the conversation feeling as though someone else is threatening your relationship.

Your Internet date should focus on you and your partner. Do not allow yourself to get distracted by other things. If your partner is trying to talk to you via video, and your eyes keep darting back and forth to something out of your partner's range of sight, your partner might wonder what you are looking at that is so important. He or she might even become annoyed at your apparent lack of interest in the conversation. Perhaps you are only looking at your cat jumping up on a bookcase, but unless you explain this to your partner, then there is no way for him or her to know what is going on.

Sensitive video

Think twice before engaging in private behavior via video. In the heat of the moment, you might think of it as a way to feel closer to your partner, but when it comes right down to it, you are performing in front of a camera. Even if you think your Internet connection is 100 percent secure, and even if you know that you can trust your partner, many other variables can turn the entire event into a public matter.

It is too easy for a screenshot of your conversation to wind up in the wrong hands. You cannot know for sure that someone else is not tapped into your Internet connection (or your partner's Internet connection), so privacy is not guaranteed when having a video conversation. For this reason, it is best to avoid doing anything potentially embarassing while in front of a webcam, no matter how much you miss your partner.

Virtual world

If you and your partner want to add a level of playfulness to your dates, consider trying out one of the many "virtual worlds" available online. These websites allow you to create your own character and wander around the "world" chatting with other people. Your avatar and your partner's avatar can meet up in exotic online locations and play games together or have conversations. Check out IMVU® (**www.imvu.com**) or a similar online world to see if this is a good option for you and your partner.

Making dates work without technology

Get creative in these situations. If your only option for communication with your partner is through the postal mail, sit down regularly to compose letters that are meaningful and help bring the two of you closer together. Consider these letters your "dates" until you have the ability to connect in other ways. The point of the long-distance date is to give you a chance to focus on your partner and vice versa, so if all you can do is write letters to accomplish this, focus on the letters for the time being. The fact that you still make an effort to connect with your partner long distance, despite the limitations in your way, makes it even more apparent to your partner that you are committed to making the relationship work.

Chapter 7

Visiting Time

Not all long-distance couples get the opportunity to have time face-to-face, but for these relationships to succeed, there has to be some time together. Even if the visits are rare, coming together and spending time physically together is an important occurrence that will refresh you and your partner. Something about having your partner standing in front of you instead of in front of a video helps you remember why you put up with a long-distance arrangement in the first place. Time together helps you reconnect with all the emotions you have when your partner embraces you, smiles at you and is just there with you.

Negotiating Time Together

It is vitally important that you both make time for each other. While apart, make time to chat over the phone, send text messages, or use whatever form of communication is easiest and preferred between the two of you. In addition to this long-distance time together, you must make time to see each other face to face. Although it is true that you might be able to maintain a relationship without seeing each other face to face, when the goal is to go beyond "maintaining" and into "flourishing," visits have to be a part of the overall equation.

Finding ways to spend time together physically can be incredibly challenging. You have to consider each other's schedules, traveling preferences and financial situations. You might have a burning desire to go visit your partner for the holidays, but then when you check airline ticket prices you find that you cannot afford the price of the tickets. You may have the financial resources necessary to go visit your partner, but your school schedule or other obligations makes it impossible to get away. Maybe you have enough money and an abundance of time, but you are terrified of traveling.

Whatever the reason, there is a good chance you will encounter obstacles that have to be overcome in order to spend some time with your partner face-to-face (or to have your partner come visit you). Keep in mind that the effort you put forth to overcome the obstacles will be worth it.

Planning a visit with your partner becomes absolutely worth the effort. Negotiate with your partner to figure out the answers to these questions:

- How often should we physically see each other? Ideally, visits should be a recurring event. Although this might not be possible for some situations, if it is possible to have recurring visits, this should be a priority.

- What financial changes should we make in order to make frequent visits possible? Travel can be expensive, whether it entails driving a few hours in a car or taking numerous flights to a final destination. This is one area where you should work together to figure out how to set money aside so visits can be frequent.

- How can we overcome any other obstacles to make frequent visits possible? The obstacles you encounter might be different than what other couples encounter, just as your definition of "frequent" may vary from what other people consider frequent. The goal is to overcome whatever obstacles you encounter as a couple and to overcome these obstacles together.

You might find that your partner's preference for frequency of visits is different from your own preference. This is one instance when it is important to not only recognize that you are both individuals with your own preferences, but also to recognize that compromise is an important aspect of any relationship. Warning flags should appear in your mind if your partner refuses to make any plans for any visits, even in the future. It is one thing to not be able to visit because of travel costs or packed schedules, but it is another thing entirely to not want to visit a partner.

If you find that your attempt at figuring out time together results in your partner saying something along the lines of "Why should we bother? Everything is great the way it is," then this should be a warning sign. It is true that some people are drawn to long-distance relationships because of the independence it allows them. This does not automatically equal a doomed relationship, but it can result in one or both partners stop trying to put forth the ap-

propriate effort to help the relationship thrive. *You will learn more about figuring out whether or not your relationship is worth the effort in Chapter 10.*

Cherishing Time Together

However, if your relationship is growing and thriving appropriately, there will come a time when you and your partner will meet face-to-face. For some couples, the long-distance relationship is a temporary arrangement. Other couples find themselves always apart, with visits scheduled whenever their finances and calendars allow. Even for couples that maintain their long-distance relationship with no real end to the distance in sight, there should be some time that can be spent together in the same room. Do not underestimate the power of time spent together that will refresh your commitment to stay together. Time together may also reveal some interesting things about your partner.

While you might be to try to pack a bunch of activities into your time together, in an attempt to make up for all the time apart, resist this urge. Your time with your partner should be as calm as possible. What qualifies as "calm" is different for each couple. Talk to your partner to find out what you can do together that not only will be fun, but also will allow the two of you to enjoy time together. Remember that time with your partner becomes even more precious when you are in a long-distance relationship. Knowing that your partner (or you) will have to leave after a certain amount of time makes the time you do have together seem all that more important.

Avoid unrealistic expectations

Whether this is the first time you will be in the same room with your long-distance partner or if this is one of many scheduled visits the two of you share, it is common for people to plan frantically for what they expect to be the "perfect" visit. In their minds, the perfect visit includes a wonderful time had by both partners, in which there are no strained conversations that evolve into arguments. Unfortunately, life rarely works this way, particularly when two human beings are involved. You can never know if your partner will show up grumpy, if you will have a raging headache, or if the two of you have problems easing into hanging out again.

Problems arise when you or your partner have unrealistic expectations for what the visit will entail. This certainly does not mean you should not eagerly anticipate the visit or that you should not plan any fun activities with your partner. Instead, what it means is that you do not tell yourself that if everything does not go smoothly then there must be something wrong with your relationship (or with you, or with your partner). Do not allow these cognitive leaps to ruin your visit and, perhaps, eventually lead to the end of your relationship. Cognitive leaps happen when your mind jumps from one statement to a conclusion, yet the two do not necessarily make sense when looked at logically. In this example, the cognitive leap is from one statement ("This visit is not going as smoothly as I had planned.") to a conclusion that is probably not logical ("Our relationship is doomed."). It might make sense in your head, but when you actually examine your thinking, you will realize the two things probably are not even connected.

Talk to your partner before the visit to find out what he or she expects, and then talk about what you expect. It is far better to discover beforehand that your partner is hoping for a quiet, relaxing trip. Especially if you were planning a busy weekend complete with a packed schedule of parties and activities and hardly any time for the two of you just to be together. Come to a happy compromise beforehand. Make it clear what you both hope to do throughout your time together, and your visit will likely go much more smoothly than it would have otherwise.

Not surprisingly, it all comes down to open communication. Talking to your partner about what you both expect for the visit can avoid a great deal of frustration when the time actually comes to see each other. Just like other parts of a successful long-distance relationship, quite a bit depends on whether the two of you are clear about your expectations, hopes and fears. If one of you is hoping for an incredibly romantic visit with almost all time spent together while the other partner is hoping for a busy weekend visiting a wide variety of friends, problems are going to arise if expectations are not discussed. A compromise must be put into place. In this particular instance, both you and your partner might be able to enjoy the visit if time intentionally is set aside for romance and additional time set aside for visiting friends.

Keep in mind that the visit is not all about you. You might fall into a trap of about what you want and need for the visit and forget to talk to your partner about what he or she wants. Many people do this without even realizing they are doing it. Even if your partner tells you to go ahead and take the reins in planning, this should not mean the visit is all about what you want without taking into consideration your partner's preferences. Plan your visits to be mutually beneficial for both you and your partner.

Accept that it is quite unlikely your visit is going to be perfect. You also may want to have some moments of reflection to figure out what a "perfect" visit looks like for you and to recognize aspects within your ideal visit that are not realistic. Do you envision a visit without a single disagreement? When two people get together for a visit, especially when there are emotions involved, there is a good chance you will need to talk through at least one or two things. Whether it is a decision of which movie to see or where your relationship is going, you might have moments during your visit in which you have to talk something through with your partner. You might think these disagreements are signs that your relationship is in trouble, but to the contrary, disagreements can be healthy when they are resolved together.

If you and your partner do not see each other often, allow for some awkwardness. Again, this is another instance where you cannot permit leaps to make initial awkwardness equal a doomed relation-ship. You are two individuals who have two separate lives, and it is only natural to have some moments of awkwardness when you first get together for a visit. This is not an automatic sign that the two of you do not belong together. It is a sign that the two of you are two individuals, and that is a good thing. Work through the awkwardness together, and your relationship will be stronger in the end.

CASE STUDY: HOW TO MAKE IT WORK

Emily, currently in a long-distance relationship

It is difficult to be so far from someone you are trying to get to know and to determine if he or she is the person you want to spend the rest of your life with. It would be nice to get to see each other more regularly. When you do not get to see someone on a regular basis, you cannot see how that person acts and reacts in situations that come up. Spending limited time together gets to be tough. It would be nice to be able to just call each other up and say "Hey, meet me here or there for dinner tonight. I would love to see you." At times, I get jealous of couples that do have the option of doing that. We talk on the phone every day, but there is something to be said for actually "seeing" and physically being with that person.

Long-distance relationships also can be expensive. Being states away from the person I am dating means paying airfares or spending money on tanks of gas to get to see him. If you are both on a limited income, it can be quite challenging. It can be stressful not knowing when you will get to see the other person again. And when you are together, you want to get out and experience all sorts of things together — movies, sporting events, local attractions — they all cost money.

Communication is key. In a past long-distance relationship, things fizzled out due to a lack of communication and a lack of a planning for when we would see each other again. Although it is important to communicate often, it is still important to keep yourself in touch with local friends and family members. This is probably important for all kinds of relationships; do not fall into the habit of spending all your time and energy on just the person you are dating. You need to stay connected with family and friends. They are your support systems whether your relationship is long distance or local.

Initial awkwardness

Couples meeting for the first time, or couples who are readying to see each other face-to-face for the first time in a while, generally accept there will be some initial awkwardness when they are finally able to see each other. For some people, the awkwardness appears as a type of nervousness while for others it comes out as a giddiness that resembles the "butterflies in the stomach" that is normal in the beginning stages of a new relationship. Whether positive or negative, couples who can accept the initial awkwardness, be open about their feelings, and do not jump to the conclusion that awkwardness always has to mean something bad, probably will enjoy successful visits that serve to strengthen the relationship overall.

Assuming there will be no awkwardness can be a mistake. Couples that have been together for a long time but that were geographically separated for work or other reasons for an extended time might struggle with awkwardness because they fear the presence of awkwardness translates into a sign of bigger problems. For example, suppose a couple that has been dating for a year and has no serious problems within the relationship is forced into a long-distance relationship for whatever reason. The long-distance relationship goes on for a significant amount of time, such as six months or a year. When the two of them finally are able to be back together, they might not anticipate any awkwardness at all because, after all, they had dated for a year. In instances such as these, any awkwardness that appears might cause alarm between one or both of the people trying to ease back into a normal relationship.

Making the best of the time you have together

Time spent together face-to-face when you are in a long-distance relationship is incredibly precious, so consider any time you get to spend with your partner to not only be enjoyable but also something that helps strengthen your relationship. When you are in a long-distance relationship, your own life has a tendency to take over, and you might find that your concerns turn to what you need to do. As opposed to focusing on what you can do to make your relationship with your partner better.

The time and effort you put into your relationship while you are away from your partner will make the time you do have together go more smoothly. The better your relationship is overall, the better your visits are likely to be. Do not ignore the needs of your partner (and your own needs) during the stretches of time away from each other. Otherwise, your visits are likely to be full with time spent fixing your relationship instead of spending quality time together.

This is certainly not to say you should avoid all conflict during your visit. If problems need to be discussed, discuss them. Just do not make problem-solving the focus of your visit unless it is needed and expected. This is not a time to surprise your partner with problems. If your partner is expecting a fun, relaxing visit, there is a good chance the response to your addressing conflict will not be good.

So, what can you do during your visit to make sure you are making the most of your time together? You already know to expect some level of awkwardness and to not place unrealistic expectations on the visit. If you can enter into the visit with a realistic view of what to expect, and you are willing to keep the lines of communication open throughout the visit, then you are setting you and your partner up for a nice time together. The trick is figuring out how to balance everything without having to put too much effort into the balancing process. In other words, you do not want to be so consumed with doing everything right during the visit that you spend more time feeling anxious than visiting. The visits you have with your partner are supposed to be enjoyable, so do not get so hung up on everything that you miss the enjoyment of the visit.

Depending on the location and duration of your visit, you might be able to schedule some fun things to do with your partner. If you meet somewhere other than your home town, you can still make solid plans for one or two fun things to do together. Even if you live in a location you otherwise would consider a relatively boring area, there is a good chance you still have a few things you can do to have some fun during your visit. Check the official tourism website for your county. You might be surprised to find a wide variety of interesting things to do around your town.

Do not forget to plan some quiet time together as well as some time to allow inspiration to hit regarding what it is the two of you want to do.

You might feel that you must plan so many events during the visit or else you and your partner might not be able to click, and the entire visit will be ruined. Instead of focusing on what might happen, focus on what you hope will happen and leave some room for things to happen organically. The calmer you are, and the more peace you are with the idea that the visit might not go absolutely perfectly, the more at ease you will be with your partner and the better your chances of having a nice visit you both enjoy.

Regardless of if your visits are frequent, or if they are quite rare, the point is to cherish the time you have together and to use this time to help strengthen the bond between the two of you. Although there is a chance that no visit ever will be perfect, you and your partner can make the mutual decision to make these visits as wonderful as is possible for the two of you. Start by deciding what is classified as "wonderful." Is a wonderful visit one spent helping each other do their homework, or is it only wonderful if you devote a day to lounging at the park together with no agenda? Ask ten different couples what makes for the best time together, and it is likely you will get ten different responses. Figure out what works best for you, your partner, and your relationship.

Chapter 8

Avoid Being Your Own Worst Enemy

Being in a long-distance relationship can be lonely. You see happy couples around you, and sometimes you just want someone to help you deal with the day-to-day struggle. Although today's technology allows most long-distance couples to contact each other at a moment's notice, there is no substitute for a long, warm hug from your partner at the end of a rough day. If you are not prepared to deal with the loneliness that can accompany a long-distance relationship, or if you and your partner have a difficult time keeping the lines of communication open, you might wind up sabotaging your relationship without realizing what you are doing.

Maybe being in a long-distance relationship is more difficult than anticipated, and you wonder if you should call it quits but do not want to be the one to pull the plug. Or perhaps you wound up in a long-distance relationship unintentionally and feel bitter that the person you love is miles away, and as a result, your attitude is reflective of your bitterness. Whatever the root of your angst, you need to acknowledge your feelings, figure out why you are having these feelings, and openly communicate with your partner in a way that does not place blame.

If your relationship is not going as well as you hoped, start by looking at yourself and your feelings before jumping to the conclusion that something external is causing these problems. What can you do to improve your attitude when it comes to your long-distance relationship?

The Loneliness of Long-Distance

Your need for human contact might differ from other people's depending on a variety of factors. Are you an extrovert or an introvert? Is you family affectionate? The answers to these questions are different for each person, and you might find that the answers differ between you and your partner. You might be the type of person who starts to feel depressed if you do not have the opportunity to hold hands and hug your partner on a regular basis, while your partner can go long periods without physical contact. Either way, keep in mind that your version of loneliness might differ greatly from everyone else's. For you, loneliness might mean doing your homework alone. For your partner, loneliness might mean going to the movies by himself. Regardless, it is possible to be surrounded by other people yet still feel lonely. The loneliness most people feel in long-distance relationships is a loneliness stemming from a lack of intimacy — not just physical intimacy, but the emotional intimacy that comes with being one half of a couple.

Do not bury your feelings of loneliness. Instead, recognize your feelings, and work through them. This does not mean it is all right to sulk in your loneliness. Instead, figure out the best way to deal with your loneliness, so it does not harm your relationship. For some people, this means writing in a journal, talking with friends, or talking to an adult. The goal is to get your feelings out in a healthy way. If you keep your emotions bottled up and refuse to acknowledge them, there is a good chance your feelings are going to come out in another way, and it might not be pretty. An eruption of angry emotion, particularly when the root emotion is loneliness, is not going to do anything to make you feel better or help improve your relationship with your partner.

Quick Survival Tip

I have a few friends who also have boyfriends who go away frequently, and we often call each other for support. These are friends that are willing to listen to me complain for a while, but then gently steer me back toward fixing whatever is wrong. I do the same for them. I hope you have friends like this, too.

As your long-distance relationship progresses, you will find there are ways you can learn to deal with loneliness. Many people find that it is harder to be lonely if they are engage in activities that keep them busy and engaged in socializing. For example, instead of sitting at home alone after school, go volunteer your spare time with an organization you care about or get involved with an after-school sport. Do not feel guilty about engaging in these types of fun activities while you are away from your significant other. A happier you will mean a happier relationship.

Always keep in mind that what works for you might not work for someone else (and vice versa), so if a friend makes a suggestion regarding a coping tactic he or she successfully used to deal with loneliness, and you find that this particular tactic does not help you, do not think there is something wrong with you or that your relationship is doomed. Acknowledge that some people deal with loneliness by spending more time with friends, and some people deal with loneliness by spending time alone doing something they enjoy. Find what works for you.

Do share your feelings of loneliness with your partner, but do not place blame or allow the emotions to grow into something else entirely. Your partner probably will enjoy hearing, "I surely do miss you and cannot wait to see you," but probably will not enjoy hearing, "I miss you so much that I cannot function, and I cannot believe that you abandoned me like this." If you are truly so consumed with grief over the distance between the two of you that you cannot function, this is a matter to discuss with a licensed therapist. You cannot place the blame for your loneliness on the shoulders of your partner, however, because when it comes right down to it, you have the choice to remain in the relationship.

You will probably have periods when you feel lonely, and that is all right. Long-distance relationships can be stressful, so there should be no surprise when your emotions seem to get the better of you. The goal is to acknowledge that you are in the middle of a stressful situation but, eventually, there will be an end in sight (when the two of you can be together), and until then you just have to do the best you can.

Quick Survival Tip

I happen to have many friends who are male, but this does not mean that I spend a lot of one-on-one time with these men while my boyfriend is away. I will meet with a male friend for coffee or lunch occasionally, but it is always in a public place, and it is never a secret from my boyfriend. You will not find me going to a movie with a guy friend or inviting a guy friend over to my house while my boyfriend is gone. I certainly could justify these things because of my loneliness in his absence, but I have to think about the perception of these events. Simply put, I do not allow my loneliness to lead me to do things that might upset my boyfriend, thereby damaging our relationship.

In a previous chapter, you learned that you have to take care to not allow your feelings of loneliness put you in a situation in which you wind up getting too close to someone else. This concept is repeated here because, often, it is loneliness that drives people in long-distance relationships to seek out companionship elsewhere. Have respect for your relationship, and do not allow loneliness to justify cheating. It is counterproductive because cheating is incredibly damaging to relationships. Loneliness should be an emotion you acknowledge and work through instead of something that prompts events leading up to the end of your relationship.

How to avoid sabotaging your relationship

Pretend that your relationship with your partner is a huge diagram featuring the cause and effect of your actions and the actions of your partner. Instead of being in the middle of all this action, you have the ability to take a step back and study the diagram on a larger scale. You can see not only where actions lead, but also what truly caused the actions in the first place. How helpful would it be to have the ability to see what each possible action would result in and to see every option for each particular decision?

You do not need a diagram to see what effect your decisions can have on your relationship with your partner. Instead, look critically at what is going on and consider what might happen if you make certain decisions. Think of it this way: Before you make a decision that possibly might sabotage your relationship, accept that you might be taking one step toward the end of your relationship.

Here is an example. Suppose you reconnect with an ex-boyfriend or ex-girlfriend online and, after revealing that your partner is away, the ex invites you out to a romantic dinner. Your ex claims that the restaurant choice is more about the food and less about the candlelight and the music, but your ex's track record suggests there might be more to this than a simple invitation for a bite to eat. On the other hand, you remember your ex as someone who is fun to spend time with, and with your partner away, you really are craving some human interaction.

Before making your decision as to whether you will indulge in a dinner with your ex, examine some of the possible options along with what consequences those options might have. Here is a possible list:

1. **You turn down the offer for dinner, and because of your hunch about your ex's motives, you stop corresponding**

with him or her. When you think about the overall health of your long-distance relationship, this is probably the best option for everyone involved. If you are trying to allow your long-distance relationship to grow (and not just survive) then the logical decision is not to put yourself into a potentially bad situation. If you think that going to dinner at a romantic restaurant with an ex who has ulterior motives — particularly when you are feeling deprived of human interaction — is not a bad idea, then it might be time for you to re-examine your own priorities. Are you trying to have a good long-distance relationship, or are you simply trying to satisfy your own needs?

2. **You turn down dinner and, instead, suggest meeting for coffee in a public place.** This option might be a good one, but it depends on what guidelines you and your partner have set about this type of thing. Does your partner mind if you meet with an ex? A good rule of thumb is this: If you would get upset if your partner did it, you should not do it either. You also have to consider whether you will share with your partner that you are meeting with your ex. On one hand, you might be tempted to keep it a secret, even if you have absolutely no intention of doing anything wrong. Perhaps you think your partner's feelings will be hurt, or you fear your partner will be jealous if he or she knew of your plans. In instances such as this, consider that privacy is not much of luxury anymore. Suppose you meet with your ex without telling your partner, and then, that ex writes a Facebook status of "I just had coffee with (your name)," and this ex does not have privacy settings on his or her Facebook account. The next thing you know, your partner

finds out online that you went to coffee with your ex. Things can get ugly quite quickly in a situation like this.

3. **You accept the offer and tell yourself nothing is going to happen, so there is no need to decline.** It was mentioned in the introduction to this hypothetical scenario that your ex's past behavior suggests he or she will probably try something with you. If you choose to ignore your intuition, you might still be hoping he or she is still attracted to you. Maybe you want some validation because you feel deprived of validation from your partner. Perhaps you want to feel as though someone finds you attractive, and you intend to refuse any advances. Or maybe you would enjoy a date, and you are keeping your options open. When you think about this entire scenario critically, however, the best option for the health of your relationship is to not get yourself into this mess to begin with.

4. **You go to dinner, hoping that something will happen and assuming you can keep it secret from your partner.** As previously mentioned, privacy is not guaranteed with anything anymore. Beyond the lack of privacy, however, you need to examine the whole concept of thinking there is nothing wrong with cheating on your partner. Even if you manage to cheat without your partner finding out, what does this mean about you and your relationship? What is wrong with your relationship that makes you think introducing deception is acceptable? If you find yourself thinking cheating is no big deal, you have some issues to tackle. Examine whether you are really cut out to be in long-distance relationship and, if so, if you are cut out to be

in a long-distance relationship with the partner you are currently with. A long-distance relationship with deceit is not going to do well. It may continue in a mediocre state, but it will not thrive.

If you can stay true to who you are, keep the lines of communication open, and always think through the possible consequences of your actions, you give your long-distance relationship a fighting chance. In the scenario above, it was when you stopped thinking about the health of your relationship as a whole that things started to crumble. Whenever you get the urge to do something that potentially can hurt the relationship you have with your partner, stop and think about whether it is worth it. Is it worth the potential pain and embarrassment you can cause to make you feel temporarily happy or validated? You have to decide whether short-term gratification is more important than long-term gratification. After all, a long-distance relationship is all about long-term gratification. You might be frustrated because you miss your partner, but in the long term, it is worth it if you and your partner truly are meant to be together.

The goal is to have your long-distance relationship flourish, not just exist. So, if you wonder why it is so important to think everything through so thoroughly, remember that you are making important efforts to ensure your and your partner's continued happiness. Although it might take more effort to think ahead constantly as to what the consequences of your actions may be, and though it might sometimes be frustrating that you have to always take into consideration what your partner will think or feel, when it comes right down to it, the effort is worth it.

Non-exclusive long-distance relationships

Of course, the rules change if you and your partner have agreed that you will not be exclusive with each other while apart. When you and your partner are allowed to see other people, you do not have to spend as much time worrying about where your actions might lead and what the perception might be of spending one-on-one time with other people. On the other hand, just because a long-distance relationship is not exclusive, it does not mean jealousy will never arise. If your partner is upset with the time you spend with certain people, yet the two of you do not have an exclusive relationship, you need to have a discussion about whether it is time for the two of you to stop seeing other people. The alternative to this is for your partner to learn how to deal with his or her jealousy issues, to accept the jealousy as inevitable, or to end the relationship. Whatever the decision is, make sure it is not fear of commitment that is keeping you both from initiating an exclusive relationship.

If your intention is to have a thriving long-distance relationship, you might find that it is more difficult to do so when you are both allowed to date other people. How can you dedicate yourself to the growth of your relationship with your partner if you also are dedicating some of your time to romantic occurrences with others? Yes, there are some couples who manage to enjoy their long-distance relationship while also dating other people, but if your hope is to build your relationship, there is a good chance that seeing other people only will hurt your long-distance relationship.

If you and your partner mutually agree to see other people while still maintaining your long-distance relationship, make all intentions clear so no one gets his or her feelings hurt. Are you allowed to have lunch with other people? Are you supposed to tell your partner about your outings? These questions probably will make for an awkward conversation, but knowing the clear-cut boundaries in the beginning will avoid confusion (and possibly also some anger) later on.

Trust and bitterness issues

One of the biggest obstacles people in long-distance relationships face is trust — or a lack thereof — particularly because they do not have ready access to each other as people in traditional relationships do. It is a lot more difficult to cheat when you're in the same town and everyone knows you as a couple than it is to cheat when your partner is miles away. Simply put, when you do not have ready access to your partner, you might wonder what he or she is doing when you are not around.

You have to make a decision. Are you going to trust your partner? Being in a relationship without trust involved can be a miserable arrangement. If you spend your nights fretting that your partner might be out with someone else, this is not a healthy relationship. Unless your partner has given you some reason to doubt his or her commitment to you, do not waste your time with worry. No amount of worrying about what might happen is going to change the situation, nor is it going to improve your emotional state. If you are the type of person who has a tendency to worry yourself into a state of convincing yourself that the worst is happening, you will find that a long-distance relationship is a lot tougher than you thought it might be. You will have to work at not allowing your fear to consume you if you want your relationship to succeed.

Quick Survival Tip

With my boyfriend frequently away, I had to make the decision to trust him. If I spent all of my time frantically trying to figure out his every move while away, I would drive myself crazy.

What do you do if you have a suspicion that your partner is cheating on you? It is one thing if you are the type of person who easily panics and makes unfounded assumptions, but it is another thing entirely if you generally trust your partner. Any number of things might prompt you to think something might be going on. Maybe you hear from a friend that your partner has started seeing someone else, or maybe your partner is acting distant and unavailable. Whatever the reason, if you have a solid basis for your worry, it is time to talk to your partner about your concerns.

Do not accuse your partner of cheating, but instead, tell him or her exactly what has you worried and go from there. For example, instead of saying, "I tried to call you last night, and you never picked up your phone. Tell me who you were with," say something along the lines of, "I was frustrated when I could not get hold of you last night. It is not like you to ignore my calls, so I was worried. Why couldn't you answer my call?" The first example immediately accuses your partner of cheating and assumes that the reason the calls went unanswered was someone else. The second example states what the issue was, explains why you were concerned, and then opens up the opportunity for your partner to explain what was going on.

Recognize that there probably will be times when you have a feeling that something fishy is going on, but, in reality, there is nothing going on at all. When you are away from your partner, it is incredibly easy to allow your mind to wander and to wonder whether your partner is being faithful. In most instances, particularly when your partner has never given you a reason to not trust him or her, it is best to make the decision to trust your partner. Otherwise, you probably will spend far too much time worrying about the whereabouts of your partner, and your relationship will suffer.

It is not always so simple. You might have a feeling you cannot shake, or you might even know for sure your partner is cheating, but you are not sure how to deal with it. This is when you need to be willing to speak with your partner and figure out what should happen next. You will learn more about deciding to call your relationship quits in the next chapter, but realize that a nagging feeling does not always mean that you are right, nor does a mistake made by your partner always equal the end of your relationship. You and your partner ultimately decide when your relationship ends, and for some couples, cheating is not always the end. Some couples can push through, but that is a decision the two of you have to make.

Bitterness issues

Another problem many long-distance couples have to deal with is bitterness. Have any of these questions gone through your mind at some point during your relationship?

- Why does he not love me enough to move closer to me?

- Why did she choose her family over me?

- Why does everyone else get to enjoy their boyfriend while I hardly get to see mine?

- Why did I have to have the rotten luck of falling in love with someone who cannot be here with me?

Whatever your situation, there is a good chance that at some point during your relationship, you have experienced some feelings of bitterness. Maybe your bitterness was directed at your partner or at yourself for making the decision to be in a long-distance relationship, or even to your situation in general. You might have found yourself bitter at friends in happy relationships with partners who are not long distance. Perhaps your bitterness was directed at a Valentine's Day jewelry commercial featuring a loving couple embracing because you knew that you would be spending Valentine's Day alone. Your bitterness might only be for a moment or it might be deeply ingrained in your feelings. Either way, it is important to look toward the root of your bitterness and to deal with the cause instead of allowing the bitterness to grow.

Bitterness can show up disguised as something else. Suppose you attend a school dance where you are the only person there without a date. The entire night you feel as though you are the oddball and have a miserable time. You spend the entire drive home feeling frustrated by your experience. When you get home, you call your girlfriend and release a tirade of all the things that bother you about being in a long-distance relationship, but fail to mention that you had just come from a school dance where you felt like a fifth wheel. All your partner knows is that you are on the attack, but if you had analyzed your feelings beforehand, it probably would be obvious that you are not bitter about your long-distance relationship. Instead, you are bitter about one night and the frustration you felt from being alone at the dance where everyone else had a date. The more your frustration grew, the bitterer you felt. By the time you got home and got the phone in your hand, you were ready to unleash a monster on your unsuspecting partner.

Quick Survival Tip

I do get tired of attending parties without my boyfriend, so occasionally, I will bring a friend along, so I do not have to go solo. It is amazing how much more fun a dinner party or other event can be.

You cannot spend all of your time wallowing in bitterness and still hope to have a good long-distance relationship. It comes down to your decision to stay in your long-distance relationship. Every day you remain in your long-distance relationship should be considered a triumph and one day closer to seeing your partner again — not a day that was horrible because of your partner's physical absence. You have the choice either to be bitter about your circumstances or to instead make the best of it by remembering that someone out there cares enough about you to be willing to be in a relationship with you. Many people cannot make that claim. Make the best of what you have, and think about how strong your relationship will be when the two of you no longer have to maintain your relationship from a distance. Successfully maintaining a long-distance relationship is not only something to be proud of, but it is also something that helps prove the dedication you and your partner have for each other.

The next time you feel bitter about your long-distance relationship, take the time to examine what you are feeling and pinpoint the cause of your emotion. Are you bitter because your partner gets to sleep in on Saturdays while you have practice, or are you in a situation where you need to learn to control your jealousy of your partner's free time? Your emotions are a choice. You can choose whether you are going to allow negative feelings to take over or if you will try to deal with your emotions as logically as possible.

When something happens

What happens if something bad actually does happen to your partner while he or she is away? If your partner gets injured, you might feel frantic about trying to find a way to help him or her. In instances when it is not feasible for you to rush to your partner's side, it can be a huge challenge to try to stay calm.

Try to acknowledge what you can do and what you cannot do. You can pray for your partner, you might be able to talk to him or her on the phone, and you can pull together a get-well care package to send through the mail. You can provide as much moral support as possible and can rally mutual friends to do the same. What you cannot do is change the past. You are probably not in a position to help your partner physically heal unless he or she is able to return to your home to recover. Do not despair in the things you cannot do for your injured partner, but instead turn your efforts toward the things that you can do to try to help.

You might find yourself in a situation when your partner's injuries are severe enough to change the way he or she lives. In instances such as these, in which physical injuries have the potential to change fundamentally the way a person lives, you have a job as the person's partner to try to help where you can while also being realistic about what you can handle.

An injury to your partner impacts you. Turn to your trusted friends and family for support, and do not dwell on what-ifs. Do not allow yourself to feel guilty if you try to do things to cheer yourself up while dealing with having a partner who is away and injured. No one should criticize you for going out to dinner with a friend or going to a funny movie while your partner recovers from his or her injuries miles away. Anyone who gives you grief about your attempts to lighten your mood during this stressful time does not understand the massive amounts of stress you are going through.

If possible, speak with a trained counselor who has experience helping people in similar situations. You might not understand all of the emotions you are feeling during this extraordinarily stressful time, and someone who is well versed in helping people work through these situations will prove to be invaluable.

Dealing with other stressors

There is no predicting what can happen when your partner is away. You might have to deal with a death in the family, a change of schools, or a natural disaster that displaces you from your home. Many people deal better with these unexpected life events when they have a partner who is there to support them, but when your partner is away and cannot be at your side to help you through the tough times, you might find yourself feeling overwhelmed.

If you are the partner who is dealing directly with the unexpected stressful event, try to keep the lines of communication open with your partner as much as possible. The more you put on a happy face and hide how you really feel about the situation, the less your partner will understand what you are going through. Share your feelings with your partner, and give your partner the opportunity to comfort you even if the comfort has to come in the form of a telephone conversation or email correspondence. Avoid the temptation to allow your grief to turn into something else. Grief is a powerful emotion, and if you are not careful, you might find a conversation that began about the stressful event quickly evolves into a conversation about how you do not know if you can handle being in a long-distance relationship anymore. When discussing your grief with your partner, focus on the topic at hand, and tell your partner how you feel. If you try to mask the emotion, it might come out as something else.

If you are the partner who is away and are trying to comfort your partner from afar, do not be surprised if you feel a great deal of frustration when dealing with this issue. You might feel guilt because you do not have to deal with the problem directly, and you might feel helpless because you cannot be there to comfort your partner. You also might wonder if you will say the wrong thing, or if you will not be able to find the right words to comfort your partner. Try to focus less on saying everything perfectly, and, instead, focus on letting your partner know you are willing to listen and to help in any way possible. Give your partner a little grace at this time too. If your partner has a little less patience with you, taking it personally is not going to help anything. If your partner just experienced the death of a family member, had to change schools, or had to evacuate his or her home to avoid a major storm, this is not the time to expect cheerfulness from your partner. Acknowledge that your partner is experiencing high stress levels and might be less than happy. This does not give your partner a free pass to say horrible things that are going to leave a lasting impact. Instead, it means your partner might be distracted, short with words, or not even want to talk.

The best thing you can do if your partner is going through a tough time is to try to be as supportive as possible in whatever way you can. This might mean staying up late talking to your partner on the phone while he or she cries. It also might mean accepting that it is not time to talk about your day, and the small inconveniences you experienced (imagine your partner listening to you complaining about getting a bad grade when your partner was just forced to move schools). You have to decide what topics are appropriate based on what your partner needs at the time. Maybe your partner does want you to talk about your day because this makes him or her feel more "normal" in a chaotic time. Read your partner's cues and decide what is appropriate for the time being.

If your partner's unexpected stressful event incurs some extra costs, this is not something to complain about. For example, suppose you and your partner have been saving money so you can visit each other the upcoming Christmas season. Your partner's uncle dies unexpectedly, and your partner wants to use the money you have both been saving for your visit to attend her uncle's funeral. Before automatically complaining about how this money was for another purpose, think about how you would feel if it was your uncle. Also, think about the lasting implications of the decision you make. Your partner might consider your complaints a direct result of your selfishness. This is not to say you are actually selfish, but remember that grief can have a peculiar way of changing a person's perspective. Try to put yourself in your partner's shoes, and try to be as patient as possible. What you might not realize is that your partner is not only dealing with the stressful event but is also having to deal with the stressful event without your presence.

Chapter 9

Knowing When to Call It Quits

Your relationship might last forever. Your partner might be your one true love, and you both might enjoy a long, happy life together filled with laughter and love.

On the other hand, your relationship might end.

Not all relationships make it, and when you add the extra stressor of being in a relationship long distance, the odds of staying together might decrease. After all, maintaining a long-distance relationship can be quite difficult, particularly if you want to hang out every afternoon, need to go on dinner dates, or if your partner needs constant reassurance of a solid relationship. Although these things do not doom your long-distance relationship, they certainly can be factors that will make it even harder to stay together.

So, what happens when you start to get the feeling that your relationship is not working? With all the added factors that can come with a long-distance relationship (little communication, awkwardness when together, opportunities to keep things from each other), trying to work through problems from a distance can prove to be incredibly difficult. How do you know when it is worth it to stay together? How do you know when to throw your hands up in resignation and walk away from the relationship and when to buckle down and do whatever you have to do to stay together? The answer depends on your relationship and what issues are making you question the commitment.

There is a big difference between ending a month-long relationship with someone you met once and ending a three-year relationship throughout high school. Although both relationships have the potential to hurt when they end, one has more of a lasting affect than the other when it comes to the damage that can be done.

If you break up with your month-long partner, you likely will be able to sum up the whole relationship to a lesson learned and move on with your life. On the other hand, if you break up with your long-relationship partner, you may change your friend group and colleges you apply to. Although you should not take the end of any relationship lightly, ending a long-term relationship should be considered an important decision with long-lasting repercussions.

Signs of Trouble

When you think you see signs of trouble in your long-distance relationship, first examine everything to make sure what you are experiencing is not the result of assumptions and leaps on your part. Is there really a problem, or have you assumed there is a problem because things are not going the way you thought (or hoped) they would?

Not all problems equal the end of a relationship. Long-distance or not, some couples fight to stay together despite problems and wind up in incredibly strong relationships as a result. It is up to you to decide what your threshold for problems is. What is the absolute, drop-dead thing you will not tolerate, no matter what? Will you leave if your partner cheats on you? Is the relationship over if your partner is mean? Is the relationship doomed if your partner does not call you every night at 7 p.m. sharp? Be reasonable in your demands upon your partner, but also keep your best interests in mind. Although it might not be reasonable for your partner to call you every single night at the exact same time, it is completely reasonable for you to demand kindness and respect from your partner.

The following list of trouble signs is not exhaustive, but it is also not absolute. There might be things you are willing to accept that are on this list, and things you will not accept that are not. The list is meant to be a starting point to help you figure out if your relationship is heading downhill. Remember that a struggling relationship might be saved, but it is up to you and your partner to decide if you want to put forth the effort or move on with your lives.

The trouble list

- Does your partner seem to be one person while away, but another person when you are physically together? If a dislike for communicating with phones and computers is not to blame for the awkwardness, this might be a sign that you are not getting the real version during visits.

- Has your partner cheated on you, or do you feel you are being cheated on? You have to decide if a cheating partner is a partner worth keeping.

- Does your partner make unrealistic demands on you or your time? This might be a sign that your partner is insecure in your relationship. It may be a sign that you have not set boundaries sufficiently, or it may be a sign that your partner is selfish.

- Does your partner not have time for you? Long-distance relationships take a lot of effort and need extra attention. If your partner (or you) does not have the time (or desire) to put toward the relationship, how can you expect it to continue?

- Do you find yourself thinking about other people in a romantic way, and you think you might like to act upon these feelings? This can be a sign of bigger problems within your relationship and is something you should sort out instead of resorting to cheating.

- Do you find your partner an annoyance? If you roll your eyes when your partner calls, or if you sigh heavily when email from your partner shows up in your inbox, consider this a sign of problems.

- Have you discovered that you and your partner have two different versions of what your future together looks like? If you are not on the same page, or do not think you will be on the same page anytime soon, it is incredibly hard for your relationship to blossom.

- Are you unhappy? Problems with your relationship can turn into a general feeling of unhappiness in your life that you cannot really pinpoint. If you have a general sadness in life, examine your relationship, and see if it is the root cause of your unhappiness.

- Is there no end in sight to your long-distance relationship? A partner who is unwilling to move to be with you (or you not willing to move to be with your partner) shows an unwillingness to make the relationship work altogether.

- Are you just not cut out to be in a long-distance relationship? You might love your partner, but for some people, the stress that accompanies a long-distance relationship is just too much to deal with.

Did any of the above ring true for you? Note that nearly all of the items in the list above are things that can be acknowledged and worked through, especially when both partners are willing to work through anything to keep the relationship together. A lot depends on your own willingness to fix whatever the problem is, the willingness of your partner to do the same, and the limitations you have set for what you are willing to accept. You might love your partner dearly, but if you refuse to accept cheating or meanness and either of those things occur, that likely will be the end of the relationship, and for good reason. Although it can be wonderful to be in a relationship with someone you love, it is more important to truly love yourself and have enough respect for yourself to set clear boundaries. A person who truly loves you will not set out to harm you.

A no-fault ending

As painful as it may be, there might come a point in your long-distance relationship where it is no longer feasible to be together. Suppose you met your partner in another country while on vacation, or you both have your own respective reasons why you cannot move from where you live. Although the two of you put a lot of effort into making it work long distance, and you have genuine affection for one another, the realization hits that there is no way ever to be together physically. Despite the feelings you have for each other, you agree that the time has come to part ways.

If this is the case, allow yourself to grieve the loss of the relationship. Part as friends instead of allowing the frustration of the situation to become a huge fight that leaves the both of you hurt. Some people have the tendency to pick fights and distance themselves from their long-distance partners when they have the realization that the relationship has to end. It is as if ending on bad terms makes it an easier breakup because there is no painful discussion about feelings. The truth is that you can never know what the future might bring, and there might come a time when the two of you can be together. Ending the relationship nicely leaves that option open and allows you to feel as though the relationship was fulfilling while it lasted. Ending the relationship with a screaming match (and masking your real feelings) only does damage.

Quick Survival Tip

Do not allow a relationship to end based on an involuntary presumption of "I can't." Instead of automatically presuming, "I cannot move to another country!" or "I cannot change schools," consider that maybe you can actually do these things.

Infidelity

Cheating happens, and when a relationship is long-distance, cheating can become easier to pull off without getting caught. Some people need companionship so much that they cannot help but to wind up in a situation where they are cheating, and others cheat because they do not feel emotionally satisfied in their long-distance relationship. No matter what the excuse, cheating is a decision that is made.

That is an important point to keep in mind about cheating when in a long-distance relationship: It is a decision. When you cheat on your partner, you make the decision to disrespect your partner. You break promises and make a mockery of your commitment. If your partner cheats on you, what your partner is effectively saying to you is, "I know I said I would not cheat on you, but for a brief moment, I decided it was worth it. I cannot be trusted."

Some couples can work through cheating, but you have to decide if it is worth it. A long-distance relationship that has experienced cheating is going to be a difficult relationship to maintain, let alone hope to grow. Consider how difficult it can be not to talk to your partner whenever you want, and then consider how much more difficult it would be if you had to worry that the reason you cannot reach your partner is because he or she is with someone else. The pain that comes with being cheated on can be significant, and it damages the relationship to a point where things probably will never be the same.

Even if you forgive your partner — or if your partner forgives you — there always will be the thought in the back of your mind that something is going on. Trust is hard to regain after this situation because it is now a reasonable worry that your partner might cheat again. That can be an incredibly powerful motivator to make you worry incessantly, and a long-distance relationship consumed with worry is not going to be a strong relationship.

There are different versions of cheating. A kiss is different from holding hands with someone else. You have to decide if what you or your partner has done is enough to end the relationship. Make this a definitive decision and be honest about your motivation. If your partner cheated on you, and this is why you are ending the relationship, explain why the relationship is over, and then end it. Do not stay in the relationship, knowing in your heart that you cannot ever get over the betrayal.

On the flip side, if your partner cheated on you, and you decided to stay because you have forgiven him or her, truly forgive and work on making the relationship better instead of throwing it into your partner's face every time the two of you have an argument. If you know that you cannot get over the cheating incident, you should not be in the relationship. If you are the person who cheated and your partner has forgiven you, commit to making the cheating a one-time mistake. If you start to feel the urge to cheat again, take a close look at whether you should be in this relationship. How can you hope to allow your long-distance relationship to flourish if you keep indulging in betrayal?

Emotionally cheating

Whereas physical cheating is a conscious decision, emotional cheating can sneak up on you. It might start as a friendship you start to rely on when your partner is away, and you slowly start to realize you look forward to seeing your friend more than you should. You start to share emotional moments with this friend, telling him or her about how difficult it is for you to be away from your partner. Perhaps you start to care about your appearance more when you know you will see this friend. Maybe you have butterflies in your stomach when the two of you are together. The next thing you know, you are admitting to your friend that you are attracted to him or her (or vice versa), but you both agree nothing physical will ever happen between you.

Is this cheating? Even if there is no physical contact between you and your friend beyond an occasional hug or quick kiss on the cheek, many people will still consider this cheating for a few reasons. An intimacy is created that should be reserved for a partner, not a friend. The two people acknowledge that romantic feelings exist, and when this happens, a decision has to be made. Simply put, your long-distance relationship is not going to work if you are emotionally involved with someone else. You cannot maintain both relationships without someone eventually getting hurt, whether that is your partner, your friend or you.

Emotional cheating also can lead to physical cheating if they are not stopped before it is too late. You might find yourself involved with someone who truly cares about you, or it might be an instance of a friend taking advantage of you during your partner's absence. Either way, if you truly want to pursue a relationship with your friend, first end things with your long-distance partner. It is far better to break things off with your partner before you do something as fundamentally damaging as cheating.

If you are unsure as to whether you are cheating emotionally with your friend, ask yourself this question: If your partner could listen in on the conversations you have with your friend (or read the email you exchange), what would your partner's reaction be? You also might wonder how you would feel if you were able to listen in on a conversation between your partner and a friend, and if the conversation was similar to conversations you have with your friend, how would you feel? Would you feel as if you were being cheated on?

Chances are that you will flirt, but whether that flirting becomes something else is another matter entirely. When you start doing things your partner would consider wrong, or if your partner starts doing things you would consider wrong, you have to wonder what you are doing maintaining your long-distance relationship in the first place. Staying in your relationship is a choice. Why choose to be in a relationship that is not fulfilling you? If you want to be with your friend, be with your friend. If you want to be with your partner, be with your partner. Just do whatever you choose wholeheartedly.

Problems Are Normal

Your long-distance relationship is not going to be perfect. You will encounter problems that need to be solved, make mistakes that need to be forgiven, and have times when you wonder if the relationship is really worth all the effort you have to put into it to make it work. Every relationship has problems to overcome, and the trick is to realize that problems do not necessarily guarantee your relationship is not going to work.

Think of problems in your relationship as opportunities to resolve something and come out with an even stronger relationship than what you had before the problem. In fact, if you are involved in a long-distance relationship in which your partner never disagrees with you and never has a bad thing to say about anything, you might want to wonder whether your partner is presenting an accurate representation of him or herself. It is much easier to pretend to be someone you are not when you see your partner infrequently, particularly when you have no mutual friends. Consider a complete lack of conflict to be a sign of a much bigger problem than having problems occasionally that wind up resolved.

How you and your partner react to problems can have a huge impact on the strength of your relationship. Suppose you have an argument with your partner over the phone, and you are so frustrated that you need some time to cool down before you can further the discussion in a reasonable way. Instead of hanging up on your partner and explaining your actions later, explain to your partner right then that you need some time to calm down and will call back soon. Your partner should respect this and give you the time you need, just as you should respect the situation and not allow a great deal of time to pass before you call back to resolve the issues. If you and your partner can have respectful conversations — even when disagreeing — your relationship will not be impacted negatively when you do disagree.

Even big issues can be resolved if you and your partner are willing to work together and be patient. This is where being in a long-distance relationship might be to your benefit. If you are so angry at your partner for something seeing him or her only would result in a heated argument, you can be glad that your partner is away, and you have the time you need to think things through.

When you have problems in your long-distance relationship, examine what the root cause of the issue is, and then, keep the lines of communication open with your partner in order to work through the problem together. Do not assume the presence of problems means your relationship cannot work or that you are not cut out for being in a long-distance relationship. Instead of giving up, try to work through the problems and see if you can make your long-distance relationship work.

CASE STUDY: EXPERT ADVICE

Reverend Michael Moore

Long-distance relationships can be a great challenge and an incredible blessing at the same time. The blessing is that the couple comes to appreciate and value time spent together because it is so precious and rare. However, the flip side of that blessing is that the couple can do one of two things: either ignore or gloss over issues in the relationship because "we do not want to waste our time together focusing on the negative," or only do the fun things because they do not have enough time for depth. The key to maintaining and strengthening the relationship is good communication.

Communication limited to emails and texts (and even written letters) is not always the best because so much can be lost in translation. Non-verbal cues, tone of voice — these are crucial if the communication is to be whole. A text or written word might be misunderstood because you are reading them without the benefit of hearing and/or seeing the individual communicating. Phone conversations play a big role in keeping those lines of communication open and with video conference tools like Skype, you can talk and see the individual. That can alleviate so much misunderstanding in these long-distance relationships.

Another key to communication is what the experts call "active listening." This can seem, at first, sort of artificial or staged, but as the tool is used, it becomes natural and effective. Especially when a couple is in disagreement, this tool helps you truly hear what the other person is saying instead of thinking up the snappy response to show the other that you are in the right, and they are obviously in the wrong. How do you hear what they are saying? After they speak, the listener has to respond back with a phrase such as "I hear you saying..." and then paraphrasing what they said. The speaker (holding the floor), has the opportunity to either affirm that the listener heard correctly or to respond in a nonjudgmental way with what they were meaning the other to hear. This is effective over the phone, in person, and via Skype.

So, how does a couple make the decision either to call it quits on such a relationship or seek help? There are some signals common to all couples in addition to signals that are unique to each relationship. There is not a cookie-cutter approach or answer to this question. The following guidelines and observations are from years of practical and personal experience.

Has the relationship fallen into a rut or an unhealthy pattern? Are you arguing continuously? About time management? About relationships with others? Are you looking for excuses to avoid spending time with your partner? Are your letters, emails, or phone calls negative or whiny? Do you have a hard time remembering the last good conversation or experience you had together? Are you, in the words of the country song, "looking for love in all the wrong places" by seeking companionship that is more than friendship with others because you believe something is missing from your relationship? Are you hiding things or people from your partner? These questions indicate significant problems in the relationship that need to be addressed quickly.

There is not a "passing" or "failing" score with these questions. However, if you were to sit down, write a positive and negative list about the relationship ("What I love about him/her" and "What bothers me about him/her"), and come up with more negative than positive, there is a problem. Before calling it quits or throwing in the towel: Often, if a couple humbly and honestly admits there are problems and is willing to talk about them with a neutral third party, it can be the first step toward reconciliation. If reconciliation does not happen, it will not be for a lack of effort.

Chapter 10

Games and Quick Tips

Y ou have the most important things you need to know about keeping your long-distance relationship strong and growing: open communication, trust, and a mutual respect. Now it is time to have some fun.

You do not have to limit your communication to talking about your future, discussing your emotions, or working through issues. Make time for fun between you and your partner even when you are separated by distance. The silliest of games or the briefest of notes can bring the two of you closer together. You want your partner to know he or she is on your mind, even when you cannot be there to say so in person.

You might be the type of person who can think of a wide variety of ways to stay connected with your partner from a distance, but if you are the type of person who needs a little help to figure out games and other quick ways to remind your partner that he or she is on your mind, use the following ideas to help you get started.

Long-Distance Games

There never has been a better time to be in a long-distance relationship when it comes to staying in touch through games. As long as you and your partner both have access to a computer and the Internet, there is a huge selection of games to choose from. Whether you want to assume a virtual life where you "visit" your partner in a world you create together, or if you prefer to play more traditional games like chess, there are plenty of options to choose from. Talk to your partner about what he or she prefers, and try several available games before deciding on favorites for the two of you.

You might be cringing at the thought of sitting down in front of a computer screen and delving into virtual worlds, even if it means spending virtual time with your partner. If online gaming gives you the image in your mind of socially deprived people staring blankly at computer screens, keep in mind you have the opportunity to try out several games before deciding on one over the other. Remember that you are not necessarily using the game as a form or mindless entertainment (although, if that is what you are looking for, this can be an added bonus), but instead, you are using it as a tool to stay connected to your partner when the two of you cannot be physically together. You should not feel guilty about the time you spend playing games with your partner any more than you should feel guilty sitting down to write a letter to your partner. You are using the games as a way to stay connected.

 ## Quick Survival Tip

Be careful with online gaming. Use it to connect to your partner, but do not use it as an escape from the stresses of life. If you find yourself staying up after your normal bedtime to finish a virtual mission or skipping out on social activity to spend time gaming, you might be developing a gaming problem. Monitor your usage and use it primarily as a way to spend time with your partner.

Conquering the virtual world hand in hand

If you never dove into the world of online gaming, get ready to be amazed at all the options available to you. There are some games in which you can create a character and live a virtual life, building a home, falling in love with other characters (played by other people), and being anything you want it to be. An example of this type of game is Sims™, a great option for couples that are apart and want to "meet up" virtually. Create your character, build your home, decide on a job, and socialize with other people in the virtual world.

Games like Sims are perfect for couples that are apart. You both create your characters and then agree on what time to log on and meet up. The two of you can then go on virtual dates, which can be anything from eating dinner together to shopping to strolling through a park. This can be good particularly for couples who do not have ready access to calling on the phone but who do have access to the Internet. It is also a good option for people who do not particularly enjoy talking on the phone or who prefer to meet online because they enjoy the format of the meeting.

On the other hand, if you do not particularly care for computer games, you might be resistant to participating in this type of online activity. If it is something your partner wants to try, or if you do not feel as though the communication between the two of you has been everything it should be, it is at least worth a shot. Try it and if you do not like it, then at least you can say you tried. You might find that you look forward to your virtual dates. It might not be time physically spent together, but it is better than nothing.

Perhaps you or your partner want something a little more exciting than strolling through a virtual park together. Games like World of Warcraft allow you to not only create a character and socialize with other characters created by other people, but also to go out on virtual missions in mythical lands. This means you and your partner can meet in a virtual world and then set off together to defeat evil creatures. This can be a lot of fun for couples that enjoy online gaming, and it can serve as time together even though the two of you are miles apart.

If none of the above options appeal to you, there are many other games to choose from that have nothing to do with creating a virtual character. If you and your partner enjoy games of chess, card games or just about any other game, look for options online that will allow you to play with your partner in real time. The point is to find something that can bring you and your partner together to do something you both enjoy.

Offline games

Maybe you or your partner does not have reliable access to the Internet, or perhaps the thought of sitting in front of a computer screen playing games does not appeal to you in the least. Many options are still available to you using other forms of communication.

Get creative about the games you play together. For example, play a game of checkers together by snapping pictures of the checkers board after your move, and then waiting for your partner's next move to be sent to you in a photo. This is a great option if you have a cell phone or even as something you do through the mail if that is your only option. The point is not necessarily to win the game but, instead, is to have something that the two of you are doing together even though you are miles apart from each other. It might seem silly to drag a game of checkers out for days (or weeks, or months), but think about what the checker board sitting on your table will remind you of — you and your partner are willing to connect with each other and work toward staying connected even though you are apart.

You do not have to limit your games to checkers. Consider Monopoly, dominoes, or whatever game the two of you both enjoy, and get creative about how you play together. The more special you can make your game time together, the more meaningful the experience will be for the both of you.

Think outside the box

Having a private game between you and your partner can be another way to stay connected. For example, set up a game between you and your partner in which every time you Skype, your partner has to guess where you have hidden an item behind you or maybe has to guess where you are Skyping from. Create a decoder your partner has to use to decode messages you hide within your emails or letters. Send trivia questions to one another based on your favorite movies or books. Send a stuffed animal back and forth through the mail that you take turns drawing on, adding ridiculous decorations, or whatever else you want to do to keep the joke going. You and your partner should decide what will work for the two of you.

Do not underestimate the effect these silly things can have on your relationship. Your partner most likely will appreciate that you are willing to take the time to stay connected, even if the things the two of you are doing are as silly as playing a three-month-long game of checkers or slowly sending a stuffed bear over a period of several weeks. The point is to do these things together.

You and your partner might be able to devise something else entirely to keep you connected using games. These games help the two of you still manage to enjoy time spent together, which can be difficult when you cannot be together physically. The effort is certainly worth it, though, because time spent laughing together is time well spent.

Quick Tips

Not every effort to let your partner know you are thinking about him or her involves a great deal of pre-planning or ongoing participation between the two of you. Sometimes all it takes is a quick, simple effort to remind your partner he or she is on your mind. The goal is not to just let your long-distance relationship survive, but to thrive.

Make an effort to work your way through this checklist of tips before you see your partner again:

- ❑ Send your partner a postcard from a place you like to visit together.

- ❑ Call your partner when you know voice mail will pick up, and leave a sweet message.

- ❑ Call the radio station near your partner, and dedicate a song to him or her.

- ❑ Send flowers or candy to your partner for no reason.

- ❑ Create a CD or playlist with your favorite songs, and send it to your partner. Take it a step further by adding a photo montage.

- ❑ Create a countdown clock of when the two of you will see each other again.

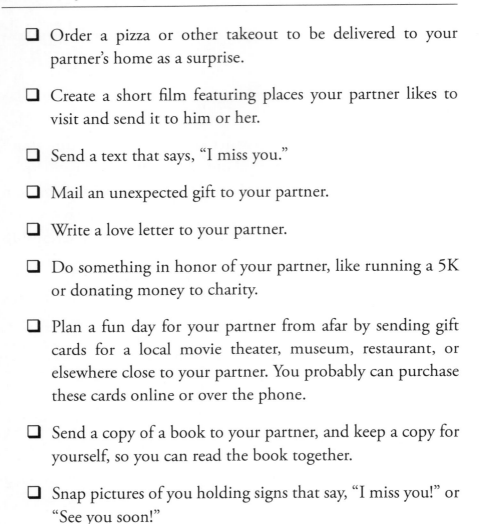

❑ Order a pizza or other takeout to be delivered to your partner's home as a surprise.

❑ Create a short film featuring places your partner likes to visit and send it to him or her.

❑ Send a text that says, "I miss you."

❑ Mail an unexpected gift to your partner.

❑ Write a love letter to your partner.

❑ Do something in honor of your partner, like running a 5K or donating money to charity.

❑ Plan a fun day for your partner from afar by sending gift cards for a local movie theater, museum, restaurant, or elsewhere close to your partner. You probably can purchase these cards online or over the phone.

❑ Send a copy of a book to your partner, and keep a copy for yourself, so you can read the book together.

❑ Snap pictures of you holding signs that say, "I miss you!" or "See you soon!"

If you have friends who live near your partner, try to enlist their help. They can assist you by arranging outings, delivering things on your behalf, or decorating your partner's locker to surprise him or her on your anniversary. They simply might keep you informed of what types of things your partner might appreciate. This is especially helpful if you have never lived in the city in which your partner now lives.

Why bother with these little things? You want to stay connected and make sure your partner knows you are thinking of him or her throughout the day. Being in a long-distance relationship can take quite a bit of effort, and if you fall into a pattern of not acknowledging your partner regularly, the connection between the two of you is going to suffer. Think of your relationship in the same terms as a pet. You can feed your pet and make sure it has water to drink and a place to sleep, but if you never take the time to show the pet affection or to give it treats once in a while, there is a pretty good chance the pet is not going to be happy and content. You relationship might shuffle along and exist, but you want more than mere existence of the relationship — you want a thriving, flourishing relationship. You have to be willing to put forth the effort if you want the relationship to be the best it can be.

The Bright Future Ahead

Being in a successful long-distance relationship can take a lot of work, but it is also something that is absolutely worth all of the effort involved. Every time you feel lonely or frustrated about your situation, try to take a step back and look at the bigger picture. You go through the things you go through, so you eventually can be with the person you are meant to be with. When you think about it, that is a powerful thing. So, although it can be tiring to maintain a long-distance relationship — especially when it is for a long time — it is a time that will help solidify your relationship. If the two of you can manage to be good together while apart, there is a good chance you can be amazing when actually together.

The Future

Why do you invest in something today? The answer is simple: You invest today, so you can enjoy rewards tomorrow. The same idea pertains to your long-distance relationship. The effort you put into your relationship today will bring you and your partner closer together and will demonstrate that you are willing to put forth the effort to make things work. Not every relationship gets tested in this way, so when it comes down to it, successfully navigating a long-distance arrangement is a huge advantage. You and your partner know you can stay together even when things get tough and even when you cannot be with each other physically every day. Couples that have never had to maintain their relationships while away from each other might not have the same confidence in knowing that no matter what, they can make it work.

Every time you make an effort to make sure your partner is happy, to making communication more effective, or toward staying out of situations that might harm the bond between you and your partner, you are doing something that will pay off eventually. All of your efforts are like investments. The more you give, the more you are likely to get back, providing you are investing in the right areas.

So, the next time you feel too tired to video chat with your partner, or the next time you get frustrated because the Internet went down during a Facetime session with your partner, take a deep breath, and remember that the frustration you are going through is worth it when you look at the bigger picture. Every time you see a happy couple walking along hand in hand and you feel pangs of jealousy, turn your thoughts toward your partner, and think about how nice it will be when the two of you get the opportunity to walk along hand in hand. Look toward the future with your partner. When you keep the bigger picture in mind, you make decisions based on what is best for your relationship instead of thinking short term and making decisions based on what you want this minute.

Always keep in mind that a developing long-distance relationship is far superior to a long-distance relationship in which both of you merely are maintaining the relationship. When a person feels neglected in a relationship, there is a chance that he or she might start to look elsewhere for attention or might stop making an effort to help the relationship get stronger. If you stop putting an effort into your long-distance relationship, your partner might stop putting forth an effort, too. This is not a flourishing relationship — in fact, it is not even a maintained relationship. Instead, it is a doomed relationship.

What changes can you make right now that can make your long-distance relationship even better? Do you have open and frequent communication with your partner? Have the two of you devised a concrete plan for your mutual future? Do you both actively work toward making sure that the other person feels appreciated? If you can answer "yes" to each of these questions, then you are well on your way to a successful long-distance relationship. Although it is true that these types of relationships can be stressful and difficult to maintain, it becomes easier to maintain the long-distance arrangement when the relationship is growing.

No Problem Is Too Big

Nearly every problem the two of you might encounter is something that can be worked through. People who successfully navigate long-distance relationships know this better than most couples because they already have faced physical separation and triumphed in a scenario where many other couples would crumble. When you manage to stay together even when you cannot be physically together, you feel much more able to conquer just about anything.

Make no mistake about it, maintaining a long-distance relationship is an admirable accomplishment. It is something that you and your partner should be proud of. Consider that for some couples, a physical distance is enough justification to end the relationship. Instead of abandoning the effort and not trying to make it work, you and your partner decided not only to make it work, but also to make it work in a way where you both feel satisfied and appreciated. Love stories are made from this type of stuff.

Be proud of what you and your partner have accomplished, and do not lose sight of the need to keep improving your relationship. If you fall into a rut of merely maintaining the relationship, things might start to fall apart. Actively contribute to your relationship in any way you can, and when problems arise, remind yourself that you and your partner already have leaped over the hurdle of being separated by miles. With this is in mind, it quickly becomes apparent that the two of you can leap over other hurdles, too.

What Does the Future Hold?

Where will the future lead you and your partner? In a best-case scenario, it will lead you to the opportunity to say goodbye to your long-distance arrangement and finally be together for good. When it comes right down to it, a long-distance relationship should be a temporary arrangement for most couples. A few couples can maintain a long-distance relationship on a permanent basis, and those that do so do so by choice instead of out of necessity. For most couples, however, staying in a long-distance relationship forever is not something they are willing to do.

If you and your partner have not made a complete commitment to each other yet, you should at least have plans to see each other face-to-face sometime soon. If, on the other hand, you and your partner are committed to each other completely, then the future should include a definite date for when the relationship will no longer be long distance. Things should be in motion for the two of you to be together, and you should both agree on how you can both make that happen.

When you think about your future together, you can be sure that by caring about whether your relationship is growing, you are giving yourselves a far better chance of lasting than you would have if you just went through the motions of keeping the two of you together. If you and your partner both are willing to work toward the good of your relationship, you will form a strong bond that helps sustain you during tough times. Failing classes, sickness, and other unexpected problems can sideline relationships that are not already strong. By working toward a solid relationship, you also ready you and your partner to weather the storms that will come your way.

Author Biography

Tamsen Butler is the author of *The Complete Guide to Personal Finance: For Teenagers and College Students*, which won first place in the Young Adult Non-Fiction category of the 2010 Next Generation Indie Book Awards. In addition to the other books she has written, Tamsen writes for local publications and writes for a variety of websites including LoveToKnow and BabiesOnline. Her two vibrant children (Monet and Abram) keep her on her toes.

Bibliography

"Exercise: 7 Benefits of Regular Physical Activity."
www.mayoclinic.com/health/exercise/HQ01676
Exercise provides myriad benefits, according to the Mayo Clinic.

Landers, Daniel. "The Influence of Exercise on Mental Health."
www.fitness.gov/mentalhealth.htm
Exercise is not only good for your body but also for your mind
as well.

Narayan, Seetha. *The Complete Idiot's Guide to Long-Distance
Relationships*. Alpha Books: New York, 2005.
This book is an excellent resource for long-distance couples.

Shipp, Sylvia Julann. *The Long Distance Relationship Guidebook: Strengthen Your Relationship from Afar.* 2006.
Shipp offers helpful tips in this book about long-distance relationships.

Tiger, Caroline. *The Long Distance Relationship Guide: Advice for the Geographically Challenged.* Philadelphia: Quirk Books, 2005.
This guide can help you feel connected to your partner while apart.

Appendix

ere you will find a list of some helpful websites including online communication tools, photo sharing and more. This list is not exhaustive, of course. You can find a huge selection of other resources online by typing "Long Distance Relationship Help" or "LDR Resources" into a search engine.

Quick Survival Tip

Resources online for people in long-distance relationships are staggering. Use the tools available to you, but remember also to turn to friends and family for support. Plenty of people probably are willing to help you if you are willing to ask.

Online Communication

Staying in touch with a long-distance partner has never been easier. Unless your partner is in a radically different time zone, you probably will be able to reach your partner every day to connect.

www.facebook.com: This social networking website allows you to post videos, photos, and status updates. You also can use this website for instant messaging. Facebook is free.

www.gmail.com: Gmail is just one of the many free email services available. A Gmail account also will allow you to blog free through the Google platform, which is another possible option for keeping your partner informed about what is going on in your life. Keep in mind that blogs generally are viewable to everyone.

www.skype.com: Use Skype for video calls and voice dialing. Many of the features offered by Skype (including video chat) are free.

www.twitter.com: Post short status updates and photos to stay in touch with your partner using this free website.

Share Photos and Videos

Help your partner feel connected to you by sharing photos and videos. Do not forget to send some print photos through the mail occasionally, too.

www.flickr.com: Upload photos for sharing online on this website. This website is particularly helpful if you want to upload photos to share on more than one social media website.

www.photobucket.com: Another photo sharing website, this website also allows the uploading of videos.

www.youtube.com: Post videos for your partner on this website, but keep in mind they can be seen by others. YouTube® is free.

Games to Share

You do not have to limit your communications with your partner to just chatting. Increase the fun factor in your relationship by indulging in some games that you both enjoy and can play together.

www.chess.com: You and your partner can play chess together using this free website.

www.mmorpg.com: This website offers lists and reviews of the latest MMORPGs (Massive Multiplayer Online Role Playing Game) available. This is a good website to visit if you and your partner want to get involved with online games together, but do not know where to start.

www.pogo.com: This free website offers a wide variety of fun games you can play with your partner in real time.

www.thesims.com: This is the official website for the popular virtual reality game The Sims.

Staying Connected

The options for staying connected are impressive, thanks to the Internet and the wide varieties of companies willing to deliver just about anything anywhere.

www.americangreetings.com: Create e-cards to email to your partner, or purchase paper greeting cards to send through the mail.

www.ftd.com: Use this flower delivery service to order a bouquet of flowers or basket of goodies for your partner.

www.kayak.com: This travel comparison website shows you the least expensive options for travel, which might come in handy when it comes time to visit your partner.

www.timeanddate.com: What time is it where your partner is right now? Use the free tool on this website to figure out.

Help for You

Help is out there, so use some of the free resources available online to make the stress of being apart a little easier to handle.

www.dailystrength.org: An online support group for people in long-distance relationships is just one of the groups offered by this website.

www.lovingfromadistance.com: Here you will find advice and tips on how to make your relationship survive the distance, a supportive community of fellow long distancers, inspiring pages including true LDR stories, as well as other resources relevant to those in "geographically challenged" relationships.

www.penzu.com: This website provides a free, online journal tool that allows you to journal your feelings. This can be incredibly helpful during times of stress, or when you miss your partner.

Index